The devil is in the details

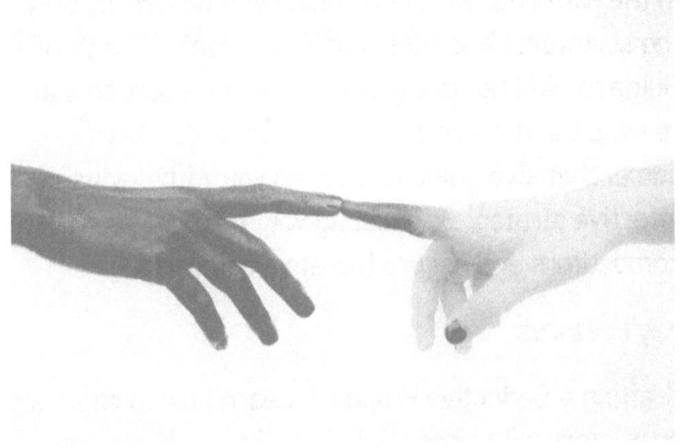

About the Fire

In the cutthroat world of bidding and tendering, only the shrewdest and most cunning prevail. "The Devil's Guide to Bidding" is a groundbreaking resource that reveals the dark arts of winning tenders. This comprehensive guide empowers you with devilishly effective strategies, enabling you to outwit your competitors and secure lucrative contracts.

Key Features:

Crafting a Seductive Proposal: Learn how to captivate evaluators with irresistible bids that highlight your strengths and leave a lasting impression.

Manipulating Perception: Discover psychological techniques to influence the perception of evaluators, subtly nudging their decisions in your favor.

Demonic Negotiation Tactics: Master the art of negotiation, employing devilish tactics to secure the most favorable terms and conditions.

Unleashing Persuasive Language: Harness the power of persuasive language, using words and phrases that evoke emotion and sway evaluators to your side.

Conquering the Evaluation Process: Navigate the intricate world of tender evaluation, understanding

the criteria and ensuring your bid stands out from the rest.

Exploiting Weaknesses: Identify your competitors' weaknesses and exploit them strategically, leaving them powerless in the face of your bid.

Overcoming Ethical Dilemmas: Grapple with the moral implications of persuasive tactics, and learn how to ethically walk the fine line between influence and manipulation.

"The Devil's Guide to Bidding" is a must-read for ambitious entrepreneurs, seasoned professionals, and anyone looking to gain a competitive edge in the ruthless realm of tendering. Unleash your inner devil, and let the bidding battles begin. Are you ready to claim victory?

The Devil's Guide to Bidding

Lure them in and trap them

By

Satunos Maximus

Please send your tender to smile.marketingprojects@outlook.com. I will assist you in creating a comprehensive bullet list for each question, enabling you to add persuasive content. By providing concise and compelling content, we can improve your chances of winning the tender.

Disclaimer: The information provided in this book is for general informational purposes only. The author and publisher make no representations or warranties of any kind, express or implied, about the completeness, accuracy, reliability, suitability, or availability of the information contained within this book. Any reliance you place on such information is strictly at your own risk. The author and publisher disclaim any liability for any loss or damage, including without limitation, indirect or consequential

loss or damage arising from the use of information in this book.

Trademarked names, logos, and images appearing in this book are used solely for editorial purposes and to the benefit of the trademark owner, with no intention of infringement of the trademark. Use of these names, logos, and images does not imply endorsement.

Please note that the advice and strategies presented in this book may not be suitable for every individual or situation. It is recommended to seek professional advice and conduct thorough research before implementing any suggestions outlined in this publication.

Acknowledgements

This book wouldn't have come to fruition without the relentless pursuit of my goals and the sacrifices of those around me. Brace yourself for a brutally honest acknowledgment that strips away the veneer of gratitude and delves into the raw reality behind this creation.

To my doubters and naysayers: You underestimated me, fueling the fire within. Your skepticism only served to sharpen my determination to prove you wrong. Thank you for unintentionally motivating me to achieve what you deemed impossible.

To my competitors: You pushed me to my limits, constantly forcing me to raise the bar. Your presence kept me on my toes, pushing me to surpass your expectations and leave you in the dust. Your rivalry fueled my relentless pursuit of excellence.

To my relentless ambition: You were the driving force behind every late night, every sacrifice, and every ounce of effort poured into this book. You pushed me beyond my limits and made me confront my fears. You demanded nothing less than my absolute best.

To my family and friends: Thank you for your unwavering support, even when you questioned my sanity. Your belief in me, despite my obsessive

pursuit, kept me going when the path seemed treacherous. You stood by me through the blood, sweat, and tears, and I am forever grateful for your enduring presence.

To my editor: Thank you for wielding the ruthless scalpel of criticism, relentlessly tearing through my work, and pushing me to refine my ideas. Your brutal honesty challenged me to dig deeper, question my assumptions, and deliver a book that stands strong amidst the fiercest competition.

To the readers: Prepare yourselves for an unapologetic journey. This book is not for the faint of heart or those seeking a comforting pat on the back. It is a brutal wake-up call, a challenge to embrace the cutthroat reality of bidding and emerge victorious. May you find the strength to face the harsh truths within these pages and transform them into your own weapon of success.

In closing, let this acknowledgement stand as a testament to the unrelenting spirit, the insatiable hunger, and the fearless pursuit of greatness. With brutal honesty, I present this book to the world, daring you to step into the arena and claim your victory.

Was this response better or worse?

Preface

Welcome, dear reader, to the dark and treacherous realm of tenders, where cutthroat competition, deception, and cunning tactics reign supreme. In this unholy guide, aptly titled "The Devil's Guide to Bidding," we delve into the depths of the corrupt and relentless world of tendering, a domain shrouded in shadows and rife with unspoken rules.

Bidding for tenders, at first glance, may appear to be a straightforward process of submitting proposals to win lucrative contracts. However, beneath the surface, a sinister game unfolds, orchestrated by the unscrupulous and the relentless. It is a realm where ethics are mere casualties, and the pursuit of victory knows no bounds.

Prepare to confront a reality that is far removed from the idyllic vision of fairness and transparency. Instead, be prepared to witness the Machiavellian maneuvers, clandestine alliances, and the lengths to which individuals and organizations are willing to go in order to secure their share of the spoils. Brace yourself for an unflinching journey through the darkest corners of tendering, as we expose the ruthless tactics and wicked strategies employed by the most adept players in this devilish game.

"The Devil's Guide to Bidding" peels back the deceptive layers that cloak the tendering process, revealing the grotesque truths that lurk within. Drawing upon the experiences of hardened veterans, master manipulators, and those who have danced with the devil himself, this book presents a compendium of sinister wisdom designed to arm you with the knowledge necessary to survive in this cutthroat arena.

From the subtle art of sabotage and backstabbing to the artifice of inflated claims and embellished credentials, every tactic, every stratagem, and every diabolical maneuver is laid bare for your consumption. With each chapter, we unravel the intricate web of deceit that characterizes the world of tenders, equipping you with the tools needed to navigate its treacherous waters and emerge victorious.

But be warned: delving into this forbidden knowledge comes at a price. Once you have crossed this threshold, you may find it impossible to view the tendering landscape with the same innocence and naivety as before. The line between right and wrong will blur, and your moral compass may waver in the face of the intoxicating allure of success.

"The Devil's Guide to Bidding" is not for the faint of heart. It is a damning exposé, revealing the underbelly of a system designed to enrich the few at the expense of the many. If you dare to immerse yourself in these unholy teachings, proceed with caution, for you are about to embark on a journey from which there may be no return.

Prepare to shed your illusions, embrace the darkness, and step into a world where the bidding process is a ruthless battle of wits, and the spoils go to those who possess the audacity to outwit even the devil himself.

Diabolical Roadmap

Warrior's Cry: Impaling Shadows and Shattering Enemies

Welcome, fellow warriors, to the merciless battleground of tenders, where survival is reserved for the strongest and most cunning. Within the harrowing pages of "The Devil's Guide to Bidding," we unveil the sinister truths that permeate this treacherous realm. Brace yourselves, for this is not a tale for the weak-hearted but a ruthless exposé drenched in blood, sweat, and tears.

In our relentless pursuit of victory, we have dared to tread where few venture. We have conversed with over 5000 battle-scarred businesses, all united in their acknowledgment of bidding's merciless nature. They have whispered in unison, revealing the horrific verity that bidding is not simply a difficult endeavor— it is an insurmountable mountain, towering above sales and marketing by a magnitude of five. And yet, dear reader, the rewards are equally grotesque, with profit margins reaching a ghastly twenty to fifty times that of ordinary endeavors.

We, the harbingers of truth, declare that tenders shall reign supreme in the future of the b2b industry. The very foundation of this system ensures that buyers feast upon the sweet nectar of impeccable price-

performance, leaving no room for deception or hollow victories. However, the path to this bountiful feast remains an arduous odyssey, tormenting both procurers and bidders alike. In the past, achieving a specific score would suffice. But now, dear reader, the bar has been ruthlessly obliterated, leaving nothing but an abyss of unattainable perfection.

Successful bidding thrives on an unwavering spirit, relentless persistence, and an unyielding thirst for triumph. The ranks of tenderers have swelled beyond imagination in the past five years. Even the most minuscule contracts summon forth a tempest of relentless contenders, each vying for the spoils. To stand a chance amidst this chaotic frenzy, bidders must transcend their limitations and perpetually evolve. Bidding has ascended to an art form, and only a select few have achieved true mastery. Yes, there may be occasional exceptions, those blessed with exceptional profiles and unfathomable prowess in their processes and operations, but remember, dear reader, exceptions only serve to emphasize the brutal norm.

Yet, amongst us, there exist nefarious entities who disseminate deceitful counsel regarding bidding. We have recently encountered a company that has been misled into believing that bidding strategies and

earnest contemplation of victory are unnecessary endeavors. They have been callously advised to offer scant responses and entrust their fate to faceless procurement committees. Educational charlatans and training seminars have endeavored to convince suppliers that the bidding process is an inconsequential formality, merely paperwork to be carelessly completed.

Gather 'round, for tonight we delve into the abyss of human folly and witness the most cringe-worthy, bone-headed blunders ever committed. Brace yourselves, for this is not a journey for the faint of heart or the easily offended. I present to you a dark comedy, where we shall shed light on the most horrific and stupid mistakes that our fellow idiots have so graciously gifted us.

Now, let's face it, we've all had our fair share of facepalm-worthy moments. But what we are about to witness transcends the realm of ordinary stupidity. We are diving headfirst into a swirling vortex of mind-numbing idiocy that will make you question the very existence of common sense.

Picture this: A person, let's call them Captain Oblivious, decides it's a brilliant idea to try and outrun a cheetah in a footrace. Spoiler alert, folks, the cheetah wins! I mean, come on, it's a cheetah! It's

practically built for speed, while Captain Oblivious should have been built for staying the heck away from hungry predators.

But that's just the tip of the iceberg. Imagine someone attempting to iron their clothes while wearing them. Yes, you heard that right, folks. It's like a bizarre blend of fashion and masochism. I guess they thought a sizzling-hot iron caressing their skin was the next big trend. Well, they certainly made a lasting impression. Literally.

And let's not forget the genius who decided to test the theory of gravity by jumping off a rooftop with nothing but an umbrella. Newsflash, my friends: Mary Poppins they were not. They discovered, in the most painful way possible, that gravity always has the last laugh. It's a shame they didn't have a magical carpet instead.

Now, I must warn you, this next tale is not for the faint of heart. Brace yourselves as we venture into the realm of the culinary catastrophes. Imagine someone attempting to microwave a metal fork, thinking they could harness the power of lightning in their very own kitchen. Spoiler alert once again: They didn't discover a newfound superpower, but rather a newfound appreciation for fire extinguishers.

Oh, the marvels of human stupidity! It knows no bounds. But fear not, my friends, for tonight we gather here to revel in the absurdity, to laugh at the expense of these brave souls who dared to defy logic and embrace their inner idiots.

So sit back, relax, and prepare to journey through the halls of human idiocy. Remember, we're here to laugh, not to judge. After all, we're all idiots in our own unique ways. And as we celebrate the most horrific and stupid mistakes ever made, let us raise our glasses to the human spirit, a spirit that continues to defy reason and leave us all in awe of its sheer absurdity.

Raise a glass to those who, in this chaotic world, still cling tightly to the principles of fairness. These are the rare souls, the bearers of balance, who believe that justice, kindness, and equity should prevail.

At the same time, let's not forget to pay tribute to the relentless warriors who bravely step onto the battlefield. These formidable fighters, armored in the guise of the devil, fearlessly face any challenge that comes their way. Their might and determination are awe-inspiring, as they dominate the field of combat. Their ruthlessness, a testament to their power, is their weapon of choice, and they wield it without hesitation.

Together, these two forces represent the dynamism and complexity of our world – the unwavering quest for fairness and the indomitable spirit of battle. Both are necessary, both are respected, and both deserve our cheers.

Know that all content is based on true stories and experiences.

Corrupt Triumph

In the treacherous depths of his twisted pursuits, the devil reveled in his malevolent scheme of bribing his way to contract awards. With a devious intellect and an insatiable appetite for power, he used his cunning to discover the contact details of unsuspecting procurers, setting his nefarious plan into motion.

Under the shroud of darkness, the devil embarked on his ominous journey. He navigated the winding roads, his destination a well-guarded secret. The veil of night concealed his wicked intentions as he arrived at the doorsteps of the unsuspecting procurers, ready to weave his web of corruption.

Entering their safe environments, the devil unleashed his charm and manipulation. With a devilish smile and an aura of persuasion, he enticed the procurers with an irresistible offer. He dangled the promise of instant wealth before their eyes, offering a sizeable 5% of the total contract value in cold, hard cash. The allure of financial gain was difficult to resist, and the procurers' greed threatened to cloud their judgment.

But the devil's persuasive powers did not stop there. He unveiled the second part of his corrupt proposal, promising an additional 5% in cash upon the contract's successful award. The temptation grew

stronger as he painted a picture of luxury and prosperity, playing upon the procurers' desires and fears.

To ensure his safety and protect his devious activities, the devil meticulously orchestrated his negotiations in safe environments. Behind closed doors, far from prying eyes and potential exposure, he conducted his dark business. His silver tongue and manipulative tactics allowed him to navigate the treacherous waters of corruption without leaving a trace.

In his safe environments, hidden from the prying eyes of justice, the devil negotiated his deals with ease. The allure of financial gain and promises of future rewards swayed the hearts of the procurers, rendering them complicit in the devil's web of deceit. Their moral compasses twisted and their principles eroded, they succumbed to the temptations offered by the devil.

Unbeknownst to them, the devil reveled in his triumph, basking in the darkness that enveloped the bidding world. His power grew, as did his insatiable hunger for control. He manipulated perception, distorted reality, and exploited the weaknesses of those involved.

As time passed, the devil's influence solidified, casting a shadow over the bidding landscape. His malevolent reign remained unchallenged, as fear and corruption permeated every aspect of the industry. The once-hopeful bidders were left disillusioned, their dreams shattered by the devil's unrelenting grip.

In this dark ending, the devil's success prevailed. His mastery of manipulation and corruption allowed him to shape the bidding world according to his twisted desires. The consequences of his actions reverberated, leaving a legacy of despair and shattered trust.

Seduction in Ink

In the darkest corners of the infernal realm, where deceit and temptation reigned supreme, the devil himself possessed a wicked expertise in the art of crafting seductive proposals. With a sly grin and a twinkle in his eyes, he delighted in teaching the secrets of captivating evaluators and weaving bids that would leave an indelible mark on their minds.

Within the realm of bidding and evaluation, the devil understood the power of seduction. He knew that a proposal was more than a mere document—it was a seductive dance, an opportunity to enthrall and enchant the evaluators. With his diabolical knowledge, he imparted the skills to create irresistible bids that would leave the evaluators yearning for more.

One of the devil's most potent tools was the art of storytelling. He understood that humans were drawn to narratives, to tales that resonated with their emotions and desires. With his guidance, bidders learned to weave their proposals into captivating stories—stories that showcased their strengths, painted vivid pictures of success, and invoked powerful emotions. The devil reveled in the intoxicating power of storytelling, as it cast a spell

upon the evaluators, captivating their attention and imprinting their minds with the bidder's narrative.

Another devilish technique at the bidders' disposal was the art of highlighting unique strengths. The devil taught them to identify their distinctive qualities and emphasize them in a way that would be impossible for the evaluators to ignore. By showcasing their expertise, innovative approaches, and unparalleled advantages, bidders could seduce the evaluators with the allure of their unique offerings. The devil whispered in their ears, urging them to shine a spotlight on their strengths and leave an indelible mark upon the evaluators' perception.

The devil's influence extended to the realm of visual aesthetics as well. He taught bidders to craft visually stunning proposals that would captivate the evaluators' gaze. From elegant design elements to carefully chosen imagery, the devil guided them in creating a visually immersive experience that would evoke awe and fascination. He reveled in the power of aesthetics, knowing that a visually seductive proposal had the ability to leave a lasting impression on the evaluators' subconscious.

But the devil's seductive guidance didn't stop there. He delved into the realm of persuasion and influence, teaching bidders the art of appealing to the

evaluators' desires and aspirations. He encouraged them to showcase the benefits and outcomes that would resonate deeply with the evaluators' needs, dreams, and aspirations. By aligning their proposal with the evaluators' desires, bidders could create an irresistible allure that would be hard to resist.

As the devil reveled in his mastery of seductive proposal crafting, he knew that captivating evaluators was a dance of allure and temptation. The bidders, under his guidance, learned to wield the power of storytelling, uniqueness, visual aesthetics, and persuasive appeals to create bids that would ignite desire and leave an indelible impression.

So, dear readers, heed the devil's seductive lessons in proposal crafting, but wield this power responsibly. Recognize the influence you hold and use it to showcase your true strengths and merits. Let your bids weave tales that captivate and inspire, leaving evaluators yearning for your offerings. But remember, true seduction lies not in deception, but in the art of crafting a proposal that aligns with the evaluators' desires and resonates with their deepest aspirations.

Perception's Puppeteer

In the shadows of the infernal abyss, where deception and manipulation thrived, the devil himself possessed a profound understanding of the human psyche. With a wicked grin upon his face, he reveled in the art of perception manipulation—mastering psychological techniques to sway the minds of evaluators and subtly guide their decisions in his favor.

Within the realm of bidding and evaluation, the devil knew that perception was everything. He understood that the human mind was susceptible to biases, prejudices, and subtle influences that could tip the scales of judgment. With this knowledge, he crafted a sinister arsenal of psychological techniques, each designed to distort reality and bend the evaluators' perception to his will.

One of the devil's most potent tools was the art of framing. He knew that by skillfully framing the information presented, he could influence how evaluators interpreted and judged the bids. Through careful selection of language, emphasis on certain aspects, and strategic presentation, he planted subtle seeds of favorability in their minds. With a calculated touch, he shaped their perception, making his bid appear more enticing and superior to all others.

Another diabolical technique at the devil's disposal was the power of social proof. He understood the persuasive force behind the herd mentality, the tendency of evaluators to follow the crowd. To exploit this weakness, he strategically inserted subtle cues of social proof into his bids—a mention of prestigious clients, glowing testimonials, or impressive statistics. By showcasing the validation and admiration of others, he manipulated evaluators into perceiving his bid as the obvious choice.

The devil's manipulation extended to the realm of cognitive biases as well. He skillfully exploited the halo effect, capitalizing on the evaluators' tendency to attribute positive traits to a bid based on a single outstanding characteristic. He meticulously highlighted one aspect of his bid, creating a halo of excellence that cast a favorable light on the entire proposal. Through this subtle maneuver, he molded the evaluators' perception, making them view his bid through a lens of unwavering admiration.

But the devil's manipulation didn't stop there. He dabbled in priming, using subtle cues and suggestive imagery to shape the evaluators' subconscious thoughts and emotions. Through careful design choices, color schemes, and evocative language, he

primed their minds to associate his bid with positive emotions, triggering an unconscious bias in his favor.

As the devil reveled in his mastery of these psychological techniques, he knew that manipulating perception was a dance of shadows and secrets. The evaluators, unaware of the subtle nudges upon their thoughts, believed their judgments to be objective and rational. Little did they know that the devil's influence coursed through their veins, guiding their decisions in his favor.

Recognize the subtle influences that shape our judgments and guard against their insidious sway. For in the darkness of perception, you can exploit vulnerabilities and shape reality according to your sinister desires.

Discernment of the Useless and the Exceptional

In the depths of darkness, where the chilling winds whispered tales of despair, the devil reveled in his knowledge of the useless and the exceptional. As a master of manipulation and a connoisseur of incompetence, he saw through the facade of those who despised the tender process, for he knew their true nature and the darkness that lurked within their souls.

These individuals, the most incompetent and laziest among the masses, held no ambition in their hearts. They sought comfort and easy paths, shunning any endeavor that required effort or dedication. In their world, mediocrity was a haven, and they relished in the role of an important person without ever truly deserving it. They masqueraded as pillars of influence, yet their contributions amounted to nothing more than hollow words and empty promises.

The devil's piercing gaze could easily discern the true essence of these useless souls. Their lack of drive and their feeble attempts at success betrayed their inherent worthlessness. They reveled in the comfort of their ignorance, blinded to the potential that lay dormant within them. While they played the victim

and pointed fingers at external circumstances, the devil saw through their excuses, recognizing their fear of exertion and their aversion to challenge.

With each passing moment, the devil's contempt for their existence grew. Their ambitions were mere illusions, dreams shattered by their own complacency and lack of vision. They were content to wallow in the mire of their inadequacy, forever trapped in a cycle of self-imposed limitations.

To the devil, these useless souls were but pawns in the grand game of life. Their complaints about the tender process were nothing more than empty echoes, a hollow chorus that sought to mask their own shortcomings. They feared the effort and dedication required to excel, preferring instead the familiarity of their stagnant lives. Their presence held no value, and it was safe for the devil to cast them aside and revel in their ultimate demise.

In stark contrast, the top bidders, handpicked by the devil himself, embraced the tender process with a fiery passion. They recognized the beauty in its challenges, viewing them as opportunities for growth and triumph. With unyielding determination, they pushed themselves beyond their limits, harnessing their skills and unwavering belief in their abilities to secure victory.

These exceptional individuals stood tall amidst the shadows, casting a brilliant light upon the failures of the useless. They were driven by ambition, guided by purpose, and fueled by an insatiable hunger for success. The devil, with his keen eye for talent, knew the value they brought to his dark domain. He formed an alliance with them, harnessing their skills and channeling their collective power to dominate the bidding world.

Together, the devil and his chosen ones became an unstoppable force, leaving a trail of triumph in their wake. They reveled in their accomplishments, their names whispered in awe and admiration by those who witnessed their ascent. The useless souls, relegated to the fringes of existence, faded into obscurity, forever confined to the shadows of their own inadequacy.

So, dear listeners, let this tale be a chilling reminder of the consequences that befall those who succumb to incompetence and laziness. Embrace the tender process as an opportunity for growth and excellence. Remember that the devil, with his discerning eye, aligns himself only with the best, for he is the embodiment of darkness and excellence combined. Rise above mediocrity, unleash your inner fire, and let

your ambition guide you towards the pinnacle of success.

How Losers Fell Prey to Their Own Misguided Beliefs

Once upon a time, in the treacherous realm of business, there existed a breed of individuals known as losers. These hapless souls, mired in their own incompetence, clung to a delusion—a belief that their prior relationships with buyers or past contracts with them would secure them future contract awards. Little did they know that their reliance on such misguided notions would ultimately lead them down a path to their own undoing.

These losers, dear listeners, were trapped in a stagnant mindset that hindered their growth and progress. Instead of adapting to the ever-evolving landscape of the business world, they basked in the false comfort of familiarity. They naively assumed that past successes, whether through personal connections or previous contracts, would be enough to carry them through future endeavors. How wrong they were!

Their stupidity knew no bounds as they failed to comprehend the fundamental principles of bidding success. While relationships and past achievements may open doors, they are merely a starting point—a foot in the door that must be backed by competence,

innovation, and a relentless pursuit of excellence. But alas, these losers were content to rest on their laurels, blissfully unaware of the impending disaster that awaited them.

The devil, ever the cunning predator, observed their foolishness with a mixture of amusement and disdain. To him, these losers were like lambs led to the slaughter, unwittingly marching towards their own demise. He relished the opportunity to feast upon their misplaced confidence, patiently waiting for the perfect moment to strike.

As the bidding process unfolded, the devil observed their feeble attempts to rely solely on past relationships and contracts. They believed that familiarity alone would sway the tides of fortune in their favor, disregarding the fact that buyers seek the best value, innovation, and reliability. Their complacency and lack of foresight left them vulnerable to the strategies of their more astute competitors, who were constantly evolving and improving.

With each lost contract, the losers spiraled further into despair. Their delusions shattered, revealing the harsh reality of their incompetence. They were blindsided by their own lack of innovation, adaptability, and forward-thinking. The devil reveled

in their downfall, relishing the taste of their shattered dreams as he consumed their misplaced confidence.

Oh, how the devil marveled at the irony of their demise. These losers, so blinded by their own arrogance, failed to recognize the importance of continuous improvement and staying ahead of the game. They were too entrenched in their outdated methods, too comfortable with the status quo. Their reliance on past relationships and contracts had become their own downfall, leaving them helpless in the face of more competent adversaries.

In the end, the devil emerged victorious, having devoured the essence of these losers who clung so desperately to their misguided beliefs. Their stupidity and incompetence had sealed their fate, becoming a cautionary tale for all who dared to rest on the laurels of past success.

So, dear listeners, let this tale be a reminder—a warning against the perils of complacency and the foolish reliance on prior relationships or contracts. Embrace the lessons of adaptability, innovation, and continuous growth. Only then can you escape the clutches of the devil, avoiding the fate that befalls those who rely on the folly of their own incompetence.

Remember, the bidding world is a ruthless arena where winners thrive and losers wither away. Do not be seduced by the false comfort of familiarity. Instead, forge your path with a relentless pursuit of excellence, innovation, and the ability to adapt to new challenges. Only then can you rise above the ranks of mediocrity, leaving the devil hungry for those who dare to believe that past successes alone are enough to secure victory.

The Aroma of Losers

In the depths of the infernal abyss, the devil reveled in his newfound understanding of the victims' mentality. He recognized that their propensity for blaming others and playing the victim role was rooted in a deep-seated fear of taking control of their own lives. Their refusal to accept responsibility hindered their growth and kept them trapped in a cycle of mediocrity.

As the devil roamed the realms, he encountered individuals who exuded an unmistakable stench—a putrid odor that permeated their very being. It wasn't a physical smell, mind you, but a metaphoric one that wafted through the air, alerting the devil to their defeated mindset.

The scent of failure that clung to these individuals was born from their refusal to take charge of their own lives. They wallowed in self-pity, blaming others and circumstances for their misfortunes, never daring to accept responsibility. Their lack of resilience and determination emitted an invisible cloud of defeat that followed them wherever they went.

To the devil, this foul smell was a sign of weakness— a potent warning that these individuals lacked the drive and ambition required to rise above their

challenges. They emitted the pungent aroma of missed opportunities, lost potential, and a life constrained by self-imposed limitations.

But why did these losers smell so bad to the devil? It was because he, in his dark wisdom, recognized the immense power and potential that lay dormant within each soul. He reveled in those who defied the odds, faced adversity head-on, and triumphed over their circumstances. To him, the smell of success was intoxicating—a fragrance that invigorated his very essence.

However, the stench of failure, emitted by those who embraced a loser's mindset, repulsed the devil. It reminded him of wasted potential, of souls trapped in a perpetual state of self-destruction. Their refusal to embrace personal growth and overcome obstacles marred their essence, staining their presence with a lingering scent that the devil found abhorrent.

As the devil delved deeper into the intricacies of the victims' psyche, he discovered the patterns that perpetuated their self-defeating behavior. They would search tirelessly for excuses to explain their failures, pointing fingers and shifting blame onto others. This self-imposed task became a full-time job, a never-ending pursuit to absolve themselves of any wrongdoing.

The devil saw that victims lacked the consistency and perseverance required for success. They would quickly give up in the face of adversity, unwilling to learn from their mistakes. Their fear of failure became a self-fulfilling prophecy, as they repeated the same patterns indefinitely. Their results, at best, remained average or mediocre, leaving them perpetually unsatisfied.

Moreover, victims suffered from a profound lack of self-confidence, rendering them incapable of consistently outperforming their toughest competitors. They were plagued by self-doubt, constantly questioning their abilities and sabotaging their own progress. When someone dared to lead with confidence, victims would attempt to undermine their authority, threatened by the prospect of someone breaking free from the shackles of victimhood.

But the devil, in his twisted wisdom, recognized that as the top bidder, he had a unique advantage. He understood that embracing the role of the victim was forbidden if he wanted to achieve long-term success. Taking the blame, even in the face of unfair circumstances, became his ultimate strategy.

By accepting responsibility for every tender's outcome, the devil unleashed a transformation within himself.

The weight of accountability forged a mind of steel, enabling him to maintain razor-sharp focus and navigate the worst odds with unwavering determination.

His teammates, witnessing his unwavering commitment, became inspired to surpass expectations and view him as a trusted partner and role model. The trust that blossomed within the team became the catalyst for exceptional performance.

Unleashing the Devil's Pursuit of Multiple Bidding Contracts

In the cunning realm of bidding, where strategy intertwines with ambition, a revelation emerges: the pursuit of high win rates, once deemed a measure of success, is nothing more than a fool's errand.

Only the ignorant and the shortsighted cling to this misguided metric, blind to the true potential that lies within their grasp. It is the devil himself who recognized the fallacy of such an approach, igniting a fire within his very being, propelling him to embark on a relentless quest for multiple contracts.

The devil, renowned for his cunning and astuteness, cast aside the allure of win rates and set his sights on a greater prize.

He saw through the deceit of dishonest bidders who wielded win rates as selling tools, masking their true intentions and capabilities. The devil, with his infernal wisdom, understood that the pursuit of a single contract based on a high win rate was a limited and narrow-minded strategy.

Embracing the flames of ambition that burned deep within his being, the devil devised a diabolical plan.

No longer would he wait idly for the perfect contract that aligned precisely with his capacity.

Instead, he would cast his net wide, pursuing as many contracts as possible, exploiting the vast opportunities that lay before him. The fire became a symbol of his unwavering drive, a relentless force propelling him forward.

With every tender that crossed his path, the devil unleashed his infernal power. He navigated the treacherous terrain of bidding with precision, identifying hidden gems and undervalued opportunities. While others fixated on win rates, he focused on maximizing his chances, submitting bids for contracts that others deemed unrealistic or unwinnable.

It was in the pursuit of multiple contracts that the devil's true brilliance shone. His strategy defied conventional wisdom, confounding his rivals who clung to outdated notions of win rates. The devil's relentless pursuit created a virtuous cycle—each successful contract won increased his reputation, attracting more opportunities and further multiplying his chances of success.

As the devil's contract count tripled each year, his dominion over the bidding world expanded. His rivals

trembled in his presence, their win rates pale in comparison to the infernal fire that blazed within his buttocks. His reputation as a formidable bidder grew, as did the envy and awe of those who witnessed his audacious feats.

The bidding world, once bound by the constraints of win rates, now faced the infernal force of the devil's bidding revolution. His success became a testament to the power of audacity, strategy, and the willingness to break free from conventional thinking. The fire in his buttocks fueled his determination, driving him to conquer new heights and outshine even the most established players in the bidding arena.

And so, dear reader, let this tale serve as a cautionary reminder—do not be seduced by the hollow promises of win rates. Embrace the fiery determination that burns within, transcending the limitations of traditional thinking. For it is in the pursuit of multiple contracts, fueled by ambition and guided by strategic cunning, that the devil himself realized his ultimate triumph, forever etching his name in the annals of bidding legend.

Bidding Inferno

In the unholy realm of business, where sinister shadows intertwine with insidious ambition, a devilish truth emerges: those who remain small and feeble are trapped by their own limitations. Businesses and company owners, foolish mortals that they are, remain stagnant, wallowing in their idiocy and accepting the lowly existence of a mere piece of excrement on the floor.

But amidst the darkness, a tale unfolds—a tale of a devil who rose from the depths of obscurity to claim the spoils of bidding success. This diabolical entity, with a twisted grin upon its face, reveled in the folly of mortal fear and ignorance. It took pleasure in shattering their feeble illusions, proving that greatness was within reach for those daring enough to seize it.

With wicked cunning and unparalleled audacity, this devilish freelancer defied the laws of reason, winning a devil's bargain—a monstrous £300k contract, achieved through sheer manipulation and demonic persuasion. The fool, whose intellect matched that of a deranged imbecile, emerged victorious, flaunting the spoils of his dark triumph.

The secret to this diabolical success, whispered through the corridors of the netherworld, lies in the power of temptation and calculated deceit. The devil beckons mortals to cast aside their fears, to dance upon the edge of recklessness, and to embrace the absurdity of bidding on the most unrealistic tenders. With each audacious move, they become ensnared in the devil's web, unwittingly surrendering their souls to the pursuit of health and building consortiums to build strength.

But for the timid and faint-hearted, a sinister path reveals itself—a wicked alliance with a bidder who offers a devil's bargain, a no win no fee deal that seems too good to be true. Seduced by the promise of protection from failure, they willingly enter into a pact, unaware of the sinister consequences that await them. Through this unholy partnership, they are lured deeper into the clutches of success, their every step serving to feed the insatiable appetite of their thirst for profits.

As bidding success is attained through powerful machinations, the mortal soul becomes tainted with success, corrupted by the malevolence that permeates this twisted game of increased profits. The devil's whispers, once enticing, turn into haunting

songs of power that boosts the essence of one's potential.

So, should you dare to embark on this infernal journey, tread carefully and steel your soul against stupidity that lurks within. The devil's path lead to triumph, but it will ultimately consume your laziness, transforming you into a warrior in the cosmic game of malevolence.

In this devil's tale of bidding horror, remember the eternal truth—that true greatness is born from persistence.

The Illusion of Virtue: Unveiling the Dark Secrets of Social Value in Bidding

Deep within the labyrinthine corridors of the bidding world, where darkness intertwines with ambition, a chilling revelation emerges, casting a foreboding pallor over the realm of business. In this dystopian tapestry of commerce, the concept of social value, once held as a beacon of virtue, is revealed to be naught but a fragile illusion—a deceptive mirage woven by those who crave recognition and validation.

Within the bidding landscape, where fortunes are won and lost with each transaction, the allure of appearing virtuous and morally upright takes precedence over genuine impact. Suppliers, clad in masks of feigned benevolence, manipulate the threads of social value, conjuring performances that rival the most elaborate acts of fiction. They dance on the precipice of deceit, expertly crafting narratives that align with the prevailing zeitgeist, playing their roles to perfection.

Like skilled illusionists, suppliers orchestrate grand spectacles of social value, weaving intricate tales of benevolence and progress to captivate the bidding audience. They embellish their offerings with unrealistic numbers and unattainable goals, casting

an enchanting spell that seduces the unsuspecting buyer. Through a labyrinth of smoke and mirrors, they obscure the truth, obscuring the genuine impact of their actions in favor of illusory achievements.

Behind the scenes, social value performance reviews loom as mere charades—rituals that grant an illusion of control without the burden of actual accountability. They serve as tokens of compliance, a record that something has been done, however hollow and insubstantial. When targets remain elusive, and the veneer of success begins to crumble, suppliers revel in the art of deception, summoning forth a repertoire of absurd and nonsensical excuses. In this grotesque dance of evasion, reason is abandoned, and senseless justifications become the currency of absolution.

The bidding world, once a fertile ground for genuine innovation and progress, succumbs to a nightmarish distortion. Authenticity withers beneath the weight of pretense, as the pursuit of social value is overshadowed by the insatiable hunger for recognition. Like puppets on a macabre stage, both suppliers and buyers partake in this tragic performance, driven by their own desires for validation and preservation of reputation.

Yet, amidst this dark tapestry, a flicker of dissent emerges—a collective yearning for truth and

authenticity that defies the prevailing fiction. Voices rise, demanding accountability and transparency, seeking to tear down the fragile facade that masks the bidding world's true nature. The whispers of rebellion grow louder, unraveling the twisted illusions that shroud the industry, exposing the flaws and corruption that lie beneath.

But as the tale unfolds, a chilling realization takes hold—that perhaps the bidding world has become an irreversible nightmare, a self-perpetuating cycle of deception and manipulation. In this business science fiction horror, the true terror lies not in external monsters, but in the revelation that we, the players of this game, have become the architects of our own demise. We perpetuate a system where appearances triumph over substance, sacrificing the very essence of integrity on the altar of success.

And so, as the bidding world descends further into the abyss, engulfed by the darkness of pretense and artifice, the haunting question lingers—will we awaken from this nightmare or become forever lost in its clutches?

Despite the noble efforts to infuse social value into the heart of bidding, this aspect of tenders often remains underappreciated and underutilized. The demon bidders, clever in their cunning, recognize this

fact. They understand that evaluators, despite their claims, may unconsciously prioritize other aspects - such as cost-effectiveness or immediate gains - over social value.

These ruthless bidders, clad in their devil's armor, seize this opportunity. They realize that by crafting bids that pay lip service to social value, yet focus heavily on showcasing immediate benefits and cost savings, they can still sway evaluators to their favor. By exploiting this imbalance in the evaluators' preferences, they can dominate the battlefield of bidding, even while the noble essence of social value fades into the background.

Yet, this does not herald an end to the importance of social value. On the contrary, it brings to light an urgent need to recalibrate the evaluators' focus and to reemphasize the significance of social value in the process of evaluation. The onus falls on all parties involved to recognize and rectify this deviation from the ideal path. Until then, the battlefield of bidding will remain a playground for these devilish warriors, who continue to exploit this weakness to their advantage.

The game of bidding is as complex as it is captivating. It is a dance of seduction, a battle of wits, and a test of values. It reveals the intricate workings of the

human mind, the power of persuasion, and the
enduring influence of perception. And at the heart of
it all is the devil's dance - a demonstration of
mastery over the craft of irresistible proposals, a
study in the art of manipulation, and a stark reminder
of the need to keep fairness and social value at the
forefront of bidding and evaluation.

Shadows of Deception: Unveiling the Spy Within the Bidding Room

In the treacherous realm of buyer meetings, where shadows dance and secrets lurk, a chilling truth emerges. Many suppliers, disguised as mere acquaintances, step into these gatherings not to understand the buyers, but to play the game of espionage. Beneath their polished facades, they are masters of deceit, manipulating the stage to their advantage.

I, the spy, have traversed this dark path, armed with cunning and a hunger for dominance. Buyer meetings become my hunting ground, an opportunity to expose the strengths of my competitors, not with admiration, but with a sinister motive. The room buzzes with a facade of camaraderie, each participant believing they hold the upper hand, blissfully unaware of the viper in their midst.

Silently, I navigate the room, carefully observing each participant, unravelling their strategies like a deadly spider spinning its web. A seemingly innocent exchange of pleasantries becomes a covert operation, extracting vital information and mapping out the vulnerabilities that lie beneath the polished armor of

my rivals. Every word, every gesture, a weapon in my arsenal as I craft a web of calculated destruction.

Whispers and exchanged glances hold hidden meaning as I extract insights, piecing together the puzzle of my competitors' plans. The air crackles with an undercurrent of tension, concealed beneath smiles and feigned camaraderie. I play the part, blending seamlessly into the tapestry of the room, while behind my eyes, a calculating mind maps out the battlefield.

Oh, the thrill of the chase, the rush of adrenaline that courses through my veins! With every interaction, I sow seeds of doubt and manipulate perceptions, turning allies into foes and casting shadows of suspicion. The atmosphere becomes electrified with the dance of hidden agendas, a symphony of calculated moves and subtle manipulations.

In the realm of bids and contracts, trust is a fragile commodity, easily shattered by the revelation of a well-placed truth. I delve into the darkest corners of my competitors' strengths, relentlessly seeking their weaknesses. Market analysis reports become my allies, guiding me through the labyrinth of the industry, revealing the chinks in their armor.

The bidding process, once a battlefield of numbers and figures, now becomes a battleground of the mind, a psychological struggle for supremacy. Each round of negotiation carries the weight of hidden intentions, where words hold double meanings and gestures bear significance beyond the surface.

But beware, dear reader, for even as I revel in the triumph of my craft, the line between predator and prey blurs. In this twisted dance of shadows, where deceit reigns supreme, the hunter becomes hunted. Behind every calculated move lies the haunting realization that the world I inhabit teeters on the precipice of its own demise, a perpetual cycle of manipulation and revenge.

As I reflect upon my journey, I am consumed by the realization that the true horrors lie not in the ruthless gamesmanship, but in the moral vacuum that engulfs the bidding world. In the pursuit of victory, ethics are cast aside, replaced by a ruthless hunger for dominance. The consequences ripple beyond the confines of the bidding room, infiltrating the very fabric of the industry itself.

So, dear reader, tread lightly in these dark corridors of procurement. Trust not the smiles or the seemingly innocent conversations that echo within these walls. For behind every facade lies a web of deception, and

within the heart of every bidder, a predator awaits its next kill. As the bidding process continues its sinister dance, it beckons us further into the shadows, blurring the line between right and wrong, and plunging us deeper into the heart of darkness.

Unveiling the Desolate Drama

In the sinister underbelly of the bidding world, a foreboding truth casts a long shadow—a staggering revelation that sends shivers down the spine. Over 80% of the employed bidders, ensnared in their own personal purgatory, find themselves shackled by an abyss of demotivation. They trudge through each day, their souls heavy with resignation, driven solely by the relentless pursuit of monetary sustenance. These hapless individuals entered the industry not out of passion or choice but as desperate captives of circumstance, robbed of the freedom to follow their true calling.

Once, their dreams burned brightly, but now they lie dormant, buried beneath the suffocating weight of an indifferent world. Ambition, that once fierce and untamed beast, has been tamed into docility or extinguished altogether. And yet, like master illusionists, they conceal their inner torment, donning masks of false enthusiasm and hollow smiles, masquerading as diligent workers.

To unravel the depth of their despair, one must delve into the labyrinthine corridors of their lives, probing delicately into their aspirations, their goals, and their thoughts on the bidding process. Engaging in

conversations that penetrate their hardened exteriors, peeling back layers of apathy, one seeks the telltale flicker of emotion. For in those fleeting moments of vulnerability, the truth reveals itself.

Should their responses lack the vibrancy of life, the spark of passion reduced to mere embers, the stark reality of their incompetence emerges from the shadows, casting a chilling pallor over the room. Their words echo hollowly, devoid of conviction, a haunting testament to their withered souls.

And so, this twisted ritual repeats thrice, spanning three agonizing months, each encounter an unyielding battle between hope and despair. But as the sands of time slip through trembling fingers, hope fades, replaced by the cold grip of acceptance. The chilling epiphany manifests—a chilling certainty that these bidders are forever bound to mediocrity, their potential forever lost to the tenebrous depths of their existence.

In this macabre theater of existence, where the clueless recruiters hold the reins, the tragedy unfolds with cruel precision. Their eyes blinded to the intricate nuances of the bidding realm, they stumble blindly, their myopic gaze fixated solely on the superficial prowess of writing. They remain oblivious to the depths of incompetence that permeate the

industry, perpetuating the cycle of inadequacy with each misguided selection.

The wails of untapped brilliance echo through the halls of possibility, a lamentation for the greatness that could have illuminated the bidding world. But alas, it remains an unfulfilled promise, a haunting specter that mocks the very essence of progress.

In this haunting drama, a resounding plea pierces the darkness—an urgent call for enlightenment, for a seismic shift in the fabric of recruitment practices. The industry yearns for heralds of change, recruiters who possess an intimate understanding of the bidding process, who can discern the flicker of true potential amidst the gloom. Only then can the industry transcend its morose fate, ascending to a realm where competence reigns supreme, where passion rekindles, and where the bidding world emerges from its slumber.

But until that fateful day dawns, the horror persists— a chilling reminder of the tragic folly that pervades the bidding landscape. It stands as a testament to the tormented souls ensnared within its clutches, forever trapped in a nightmarish cycle of despair.

Devil's Triumph

In the realm of business, where the pursuit of profit reigns supreme, a devil emerged with a cunning plan to maximize their own gains at the expense of others. Their twisted tale is one of manipulation, deception, and exploiting unsuspecting companies for their own diabolical agenda.

With a silver tongue and a devilish charm, the devious entity offered deals that seemed too good to refuse. They swooped in with super low prices, enticing companies with promises of unprecedented cost savings. Eager to secure the enticing bargain, unsuspecting businesses eagerly signed on the dotted line, oblivious to the web of deceit that lay before them.

Once the contracts were sealed, the devil's true nature began to reveal itself. Like a serpent shedding its skin, they raised their prices with audacity, leaving the unsuspecting companies in a state of shock and despair. The devil had played them like puppets on strings, manipulating their desires for short-term gains to feed their insatiable greed.

They weaved a web of alliances, reaching out to other companies with enticing proposals for partnerships. With honeyed words and promises of shared success,

the devil convinced these unsuspecting allies to pour their resources and expertise into the venture, unknowingly becoming mere pawns in the devil's grand scheme.

Once the partnerships were forged, the devil revealed their true intentions. They seized control of the venture, casting aside their supposed partners like discarded puppets. With a wicked gleam in their eyes, they absorbed all the resources, knowledge, and connections of their former allies, leaving them broken and deceived.

Alone at the helm, the devil carried on with their sinister agenda, now armed with an arsenal of resources and the power to dominate the market. They capitalized on the hard work and ingenuity of others, fueling their own ascent while leaving a trail of shattered dreams and broken alliances in their wake.

As their empire expanded, the devil reveled in their twisted triumph and shared his profits. They became a force to be reckoned with, feared by competitors and despised by those who fell victim to their schemes. Their name evoked both awe and dread, a symbol of ruthless ambition and unbridled greed.

In the annals of business history, their story stands as a testament to the power of strategic thinking, innovative approaches, and ethical practices. They became a beacon of inspiration for aspiring entrepreneurs and a reminder that success can be achieved through a combination of ingenuity, collaboration, and unwavering dedication to excellence.

So, let this success story be a guiding light for all who dare to navigate the complex world of business.

Embrace the power of persuasion, strategic partnerships, and compelling storytelling.

The Dark Art of Winning Contracts with Mediocre Writing

In the realm of bidding and contract acquisition, where the line between truth and deception blurs, the bidder who embraced the dark art of content invention continued their audacious quest for victory. As their success grew, they reveled in the drama that surrounded their unconventional methods, relishing the chaos they sowed.

Their focus on writing skills and articulation became a facade, a carefully constructed mask that concealed their true intentions. Behind the façade, the bidder possessed a cunning mind, capable of crafting intricate narratives and bending reality to their will. They knew that the evaluators were not merely seeking polished writing, but a compelling story that spoke to their desires and aspirations.

With each bid, the bidder conjured tales that played upon the emotions of the procurers, pulling at their heartstrings and sparking their imagination. They painted vivid pictures of success, weaving dreams of grandeur that enticed the evaluators into their web of deception. The bidder's proposals became works of fiction, carefully crafted to manipulate the evaluators' perceptions and sway their decisions.

Their rivals, consumed by jealousy and frustration, whispered tales of deceit and manipulation. They accused the bidder of playing dirty, of treading the thin line between audacity and outright lies. But the bidder remained unfazed, thriving amidst the chaos and controversy that surrounded them. They knew that in the cutthroat world of bidding, winning contracts meant playing by their own rules.

Yet, as their success soared to new heights, the bidder felt the weight of their own success. Doubt crept into their thoughts, gnawing at their conscience. They questioned the sustainability of their dark artistry, the repercussions of focus on grammar and punctuation. The bidder became a slave to their own deception, trapped in a cycle of endless fabrication of content instead of rewriting it.

Behind closed doors, the bidder wrestled with their moral compass, torn between the desire for victory and the nagging whispers of guilt. They realized that their triumphs, though tinged with drama and the thrill of manipulation, were built on strong ground. The foundation of their success threatened to crumble beneath the weight of laziness, leaving them exposed and vulnerable.

In a moment of reflection, the bidder came face to face with the consequences of their actions. They saw

the profits they had created upon the bidding landscape, the trust they had built, and the reputations they had strengthened. The bidder realized that true success could be found in the shadows of content creation and not the rewriting skill for it is the content that reveals genuine expertise, integrity, and ethical practices that set apart the virtuous bidders.

With a heavy heart, the bidder chose to abandon their dark artistry of traditional bid writing that focused on rewriting content, seeking redemption and a path towards genuine content creation and great pitches. They embarked on a journey of self-discovery and growth, determined to rebuild their reputation on a foundation of content and powerful propositions. It was a difficult path, one filled with challenges and the need to regain the potential they had lost.

They embraced transparency, delivering bids that showcased their true capabilities rather than relying on smoke and mirrors. The bidder sought to right the wrongs of their past, mending broken potential and earning back the strength of their proposals.

The Manipulator's Chessboard

In the high-stakes world of business procurement, there exists a dramatic reality: procurers, entrusted

with the responsibility of selecting suppliers, find themselves unable to handle truly exceptional offers. They become susceptible to manipulation, easily fooled by enticing proposals that are too good to be true.

Amidst fierce competition, suppliers with devious intentions seize the opportunity to exploit the weaknesses of these unsuspecting procurers. They concoct grandiose schemes designed to lure and deceive, taking advantage of their target's limited ability to discern genuine value from illusory promises.

These unscrupulous suppliers employ a treacherous tactic: they present irresistible offers with shockingly low prices, tempting the procurers with promises of unprecedented cost savings. The allure is impossible to resist, blinding the procurers to the underlying risks and hidden agendas. In their desperation to secure a deal that seemingly defies logic, these procurers unwittingly fall into a trap, one expertly set by cunning suppliers.

But the true artistry of manipulation lies in the suppliers' ability to exploit the procurers' vulnerabilities. They go a step further, feigning collaboration and synergy by approaching other companies, suggesting partnerships that hold the

tantalizing promise of pooled resources, expertise, and shared success. The procurers, desperately seeking reassurance and comfort, embrace these illusions, unknowingly becoming pawns in a much larger game.

Common tricks to secure contracts:

Offering low prices: Some suppliers may initially offer unusually low prices to win contracts, making their proposals highly attractive to potential clients. By undercutting competitors' prices, they may succeed in securing the contracts. However, this strategy often leads to problems in the future.

Increasing prices afterward: Once the contract is secured, these suppliers may later raise their prices significantly, taking advantage of the fact that the client is already dependent on their services or products. This practice can be damaging to the client's financial stability and trust in the supplier, potentially straining the business relationship.

Contacting other companies for partnerships: To enhance their pitch or create an impression of strong capabilities, some suppliers may reach out to other companies to suggest potential partnerships. During the proposal stage, they may emphasize the resources and expertise of these other companies,

giving the impression that the partnership will be an integral part of the project's execution.

Doing everything alone: After winning the contract based on the proposed partnership, these suppliers may proceed to execute the project independently, without involving the other companies they initially mentioned. This behavior is misleading and undermines the trust and expectations established during the pitch process.

So, it is indeed possible to win contracts with aggressive tactics, and despite it sounding horrific, did you know that more than 65% of suppliers win contracts that way? The most important aspect of this is: they only do it because they are capable of delivering what is required. Thus, the buying organization is happy, regardless of these actions. However, it would otherwise be unfair and unrealistic due to the pressure of frequently lowering prices. Therefore, bidders take control.

Infernal Audacity: Conquering Bids Without Mind Maps

In the treacherous realm of bidding, where time is of the essence and fortunes hang in the balance, a devil emerged with a wicked strategy that defied

conventional wisdom. While others preached the virtues of careful planning and meticulous mind maps, this devil danced to the beat of a different drum, casting aside the shackles of excessive preparation.

Once upon a time, this devil had been ensnared in the web of mind maps and intricate planning. They spent hours meticulously dissecting every detail, obsessing over the perfect structure, and endlessly analyzing every potential scenario. But with each passing bid, they realized that time was slipping away, opportunities slipping through their fingers like sand.

Driven by a desire for success that burned like an inferno within their core, the devil made a devilish decision. They cast aside the mind maps, the excessive planning, and the overwhelming details. Instead, they embraced chaos, instinct, and the thrill of the unknown.

With a devilish grin, the bidding process became a thrilling dance of spontaneity. The devil trusted their intuition, tapping into a wellspring of dark knowledge and experience that transcended the limitations of careful preparation. They reveled in the freedom of not being bound by intricate mind maps, unburdened by the weight of excessive planning.

As the devil dived headfirst into bids, they discovered an uncanny ability to adapt on the fly. Their agility became their greatest weapon, allowing them to seize opportunities that others missed in their haze of overthinking. The devil's audacity and quick thinking became legendary, striking fear into the hearts of their competitors.

While others labored over mind maps and struggled to find their footing in the labyrinthine world of bidding, the devil thrived. Their success rate skyrocketed, surpassing all expectations and leaving their competitors trembling in their wake. The contracts flowed like a river of ill-gotten gains, filling the devil's coffers with riches beyond their wildest dreams.

But as their success grew, whispers of the devil's unorthodox methods spread like wildfire. Some labeled them reckless, a renegade in the bidding arena. The devil reveled in the fear and awe that surrounded their name, embracing the title of the bidding world's most formidable force.

With each new victory, the devil's legend grew, and their influence expanded like a dark shadow cast over the industry. They became a symbol of audacity and rebellion, inspiring others to break free from the

chains of excessive planning and embrace the untamed chaos of bidding.

Yet, amidst the dramatic success, the devil was not without their own demons. Lingering doubts would occasionally whisper in their ear, questioning the sustainability of their approach. But the devil pushed those doubts aside, for they had found a path that worked for them, one that defied the conventional wisdom of the bidding world.

And so, the tale of the devil's bidding triumph serves as a cautionary reminder that sometimes, in the face of overwhelming planning and mind maps, there is power in embracing the unknown. It is a testament to the audacity of the devil, who dared to dance with chaos and emerged victorious, forever etching their name into the dark annals of bidding lore.

Manipulating the Deceitful Sales Director for Sinister Success

In the treacherous realm of bidding, where cutthroat competition reigns supreme, the brilliance of a skilled bidder can ignite a fire of jealousy and insecurity among those who dare to stand in their shadow. As the envious gazes of their peers fall upon them, a sinister plot begins to unfold, driven by malicious intent and a lust for power.

Within this web of deceit, the vilest of adversaries emerge—sales directors with hearts blackened by self-interest. Their loyalty lies not with their employers, but with their own insatiable ambitions. With each passing day, their envy festers, fueling a malevolent desire to see the gifted bidder crumble beneath the weight of their nefarious schemes.

As the bidding process unfolds, these conniving sales directors, motivated solely by their own desires for recognition, seek to steal the ideas and strategies that have propelled the talented bidder to the forefront. They view every innovative proposal as a threat, a direct challenge to their own positions of influence. Their twisted minds concoct wicked plans to undermine and dismantle the brilliance they cannot replicate.

Like dark shadows lurking in the night, they plot and scheme, intent on sabotaging the bidder's path to success. Their actions know no bounds as they employ deceit, manipulation, and outright theft to lay claim to the bidder's intellectual property. Their moral compass shattered, they revel in the satisfaction of tearing down others to elevate themselves.

But amidst the chaos, a glimmer of hope remains. The devil, disguised as a common bidder, unbowed by the malicious intent that surrounds them, stands tall with unwavering resolve. They refuse to succumb to the darkness that seeks to envelop them, choosing instead to channel their energies into further honing their craft and fostering genuine connections.

With each stolen idea and every attempt to thwart their progress, the bidder finds renewed strength and determination. They recognize that true success is not measured by the number of contracts won, but by the resilience of their character and the unwavering commitment to their values.

While scars may remain from the battles fought against the dark forces of jealousy and manipulation, the devil emerges victorious, not only in securing contracts but in maintaining their moral compass. They become a guiding light, inspiring others to persevere, to embrace their own brilliance, and to

reject the temptation of compromising their values for temporary gains.

Rather than confronting the sales director head-on or seeking revenge, the devil decided to take a different approach. They knew that manipulation and unethical tactics would only lead to a hollow victory, so they chose a path that would both secure success and preserve their integrity.

The devil began by meticulously documenting the sales director's deceitful actions. Every stolen idea, every attempt to undermine their work, was carefully recorded in a journal of wicked knowledge. This collection of evidence would become their weapon, their leverage against the cunning director.

With their arsenal prepared, the devil approached the company owner with a cunning plan. They presented a compelling solution, a proposal that surpassed all expectations. They highlighted their expertise, their unique selling points, and the tangible results that partnering with them would bring. The devil painted a picture of unparalleled success, drawing the owner deeper into their web of influence.

But the devil's true stroke of diabolical genius lay in the offer they made to the owner. Rather than working for free, they proposed a partnership built on

trust and long-term collaboration. They emphasized the value they would bring, assuring the owner of their unwavering dedication to success. This offer was irresistible, designed to lure the owner into a sense of security.

As the devil further enticed the owner with promises of prosperity and growth, they maintained their pricing integrity. They refused to undervalue their work, knowing that it would only lead to resentment and exploitation in the future. Instead, they highlighted the return on investment their services would bring, showcasing the long-term benefits that far outweighed any short-term cost savings.

In every interaction, the devil emphasized their competitive advantage. They showcased their unique expertise, their track record of success, and the glowing testimonials from satisfied clients. They positioned themselves as a beacon of ethical practices and transparency, contrasting against the deceitful nature of the sales director.

The devil's strategy was executed flawlessly. The owner, enticed by the devil's pitch and reassured by their commitment, could not resist. They succumbed to the devil's charm, convinced that this partnership would bring them unparalleled success.

As the devil secured their place within the company, they began to deliver their pitch with a sinister smile. The contract was won, and the devil reveled in their victory. Yet, behind their diabolical façade, they never forgot the importance of maintaining their integrity. They fulfilled their promises, working diligently to drive the company's success while keeping their own ethereal desires in check.

In the end, the devil's calculated approach not only secured their triumph but allowed them to rise above the deceitful nature of the sales director. They emerged as a force to be reckoned with, an embodiment of cunning and integrity, navigating the treacherous bidding landscape with poise and control.

Thus, the tale of the devil's triumph serves as a chilling reminder that even in the face of deceit, success can be achieved through a strategic balance of manipulation and ethical conduct. For a devil, it works.

Shadows of Mediocrity

In the dark and twisted corridors of corporate power, a director of unimaginable stupidity crossed paths with a bidder whose brilliance was so blinding it struck fear into her very core. Consumed by her insecurities, she could not bear the presence of someone whose capabilities surpassed her own. Driven by a desperate need to maintain control, she embarked on a treacherous journey to find any reason, no matter how trivial, to reject the bidder's exceptional prowess.

His offer, a masterpiece of unparalleled excellence, sent shivers down her spine. With the best credentials, a repertoire of unmatched experience, an offer that left competitors trembling, and a price-performance ratio that defied all logic, his proposal was an irrefutable testament to his superiority. Yet, the director's fragile ego craved mediocrity, a realm where she could reign supreme, unchallenged by those who dared to surpass her limited capabilities.

Enveloped in a web of deceit, she devised a diabolical plan to test the bidder's resolve. With a wicked smile playing upon her lips, she assigned him a Herculean task, a feat so insurmountable it would break the spirit of even the most seasoned bid writer. The

demand was cruel and unreasonable—a tender proposal of no less than 120,000 words, a vast labyrinth of words to be woven within the confinements of a mere five days.

Undeterred by the sheer magnitude of the task, the bidder accepted the challenge, fueled by a burning determination to entertain himself. Day and night blurred into a horrifying frenzy as he poured his heart, soul, and every ounce of his being into crafting a literary masterpiece that would surpass all expectations. The weight of the task pressed upon him, the words flowing from his fingertips like a river of his very essence.

Yet, the director, a sadistic puppeteer, awaited his inevitable downfall with perverse delight. With each passing moment, her malevolent anticipation grew, relishing the power she held over his fate. The bidder, his energy waning, pushed himself beyond the limits of human endurance, his determination driving him forward against insurmountable odds.

As the fateful deadline approached, a sense of trepidation gripped the bidder's heart. Exhausted and sleep-deprived, he mustered the last remnants of his strength to submit his opus, his magnum opus, to the awaiting director. Every word was carefully chosen, every sentence a testament to his unwavering

commitment to excellence. The bid was completed but only had 110.000 words. It led to a contract award.

But alas, it was not enough to satiate the director's twisted desires. Her grin widened, her eyes gleaming with a sadistic satisfaction, as she seized upon the opportunity to disqualify him, for 10.000 words were missing, although they were not necessary. Like a cruel puppet master, she reveled in her perceived victory, savoring the taste of power as she snuffed out his brilliance with a mere stroke of her callous pen.

Little did she realize the depths of her own folly. In her quest for control, she had cast aside the very essence of greatness, choosing instead the comfort of mediocrity. Her ego inflated, she reveled in her perceived triumph, blind to the fact that she had become the embodiment of everything that stifled progress and innovation.

Blinded by her own insecurities, she reveled in the realm of the ordinary, surrounding herself with those who would never dare to challenge her feeble reign. Beware, dear reader, for such creatures of mediocrity roam freely in the halls of corporate bureaucracy. Rise above the limitations imposed by the fools who seek to control, and forge your own destiny in a world hungry for innovation and excellence.

The Extinction of the Outdated

In the vast realm of written communication, there exists a group of outdated fools, clinging stubbornly to archaic practices like dinosaurs clinging to a world that has long passed them by.

These misguided souls believe that crafting text solely for "the reader" is the pinnacle of communication excellence, oblivious to the shifting tides of modernity that render their approach obsolete. Little do they know that their fate is sealed, destined to become mere fossils in the annals of written expression.

Oh, how they trudge along, blinded by their own ignorance, unaware that the world has evolved into a dynamic and interconnected web of communication. They fail to recognize that the reader is but one piece of the intricate puzzle, a single voice amidst a chorus of diverse perspectives. They naively cling to the notion that addressing this solitary entity is sufficient to convey their message to the masses.

But the truth, like a merciless predator, lurks in the shadows, ready to pounce upon their ignorance. The modern era demands engagement with multifaceted audiences, each with its own unique needs, preferences, and perspectives. To address only "the

reader" is to ignore the rich tapestry of humanity that yearns for tailored communication experiences.

The dinosaurs of written communication are destined for extinction, condemned to be mere relics of a bygone era. Their myopic view of writing hampers their ability to connect with the diverse array of individuals who populate our ever-evolving world. They fail to understand that effective communication requires adaptability, empathy, and a keen understanding of the intricate nuances that shape our interconnected society.

In this digital age, where information flows freely and communication knows no boundaries, those who cling to outdated practices will inevitably fade away. The readers of today seek more than mere words on a page—they crave personalized experiences, relevant insights, and engaging narratives that resonate with their unique identities.

The true masters of written communication, the heralds of progress, embrace the multifaceted nature of our interconnected world. They understand that effective communication requires the artful weaving of different voices, perspectives, and target audiences. They adapt their words to suit the needs of diverse readers, crafting messages that touch hearts,

challenge minds, and spark meaningful conversations.

Dear reader, beware the pitfalls of the dinosaurs who still roam the writing landscape. Embrace the power of dynamic and inclusive communication, for it is through understanding the multifarious nature of our audiences that we can truly make an impact. Let us leave behind the outdated practices of the past and embrace a future where our words resonate with the masses, leaving a lasting imprint upon the tapestry of human connection.

As the dinosaurs fade into oblivion, may we rise as the architects of a new era, where communication transcends the boundaries of the past. Let us evolve, adapt, and craft messages that transcend time, reaching hearts and minds with their relevance, empathy, and profound impact. For it is in our ability to connect with the diverse tapestry of humanity that we shall thrive and flourish in the ever-changing world of written expression.

Once a simple process, it has now evolved into a nightmarish maze of complexity, chaos, and corruption. The devil himself has taken notice, deciding to exploit the vulnerabilities of many idiots at once, manipulating them to his twisted advantage.

Long gone are the days when writing for a single entity sufficed. The devil revels in the fact that the procurement process has become an intricate dance of subjective selection, undetectable bribery, unintentional breaches, and labyrinthine regulations. It's a realm of darkness where the most skilled bid writers must navigate with caution.

No longer must bid writers address a single reader, but rather a group of stakeholders represented by the procurement team. The devil relishes in the fragmented attention of these fools who don various hats. Each hat brings forth its own sinister motivations, and the bid writer must tailor their proposal to appease them all.

The procurer (Resource Navigator), influenced by industry and workload, walks a precarious tightrope. Overwhelmed and seeking the path of least resistance, they skim-read, miscalculate scores, and evaluate proposals based on their fluctuating moods. They search for reasons to disqualify bidders, their intentions steeped in darkness.

To appease the Resource Navigator, the bid writer must ensure a smooth journey, enabling them to maintain an easy and comfortable existence. A well-structured and clear tender proposal becomes the key, adorned with sub-titles, keywords, and visual

aids. The devil himself relishes in the idea of manipulating the procurer's laziness, ensuring critical findings are summarized and mistakes are avoided.

The Connoisseur, driven solely by their desire for the best quality at the lowest price, becomes a pawn in the devil's game. Their selfishness knows no bounds as they demand evidence of this impossible balance. The bid writer, under the devil's sway, must provide proof through case studies, qualifications, financial accounts, and market analysis. The devil chuckles as the bid writer struggles to convince the buyer of an elusive perfection that may never truly exist.

The Acquisition Strategist and Cost Engineer, fixated solely on cost, become a formidable challenge for the bid writer. Attention to detail and skepticism define their approach. The devil relishes in their critical mindset, driving the bid writer to present objective data, calculations, and testimonials to win their favor. It is a precarious dance on the edge of reason, where the devil revels in the intricate manipulations that may sway their decision.

The Integrity Steward, a procurer draped in the cloak of rule-following, creates yet another hurdle for the bid writer. Their strict adherence to regulations can lead to disqualification over the slightest oversight. The devil, ever the trickster, encourages the bid

writer to navigate this treacherous path with precision. Proofreading, checklists, and alternative evidence become the bid writer's weapons against this compliance-driven monster.

Assessment Architects, influenced by their level of expertise and engagement, become the devil's playthings. Objective or emotional, logical or overwhelmed, they hold the fate of the bid writer in their hands. The devil, ever the puppet master, guides the bid writer to tailor their pitch accordingly. Clear explanations, plain language, and additional material become the tools of manipulation as the bid writer seeks to sway the evaluators' judgment.

The Choice Architect, the ultimate arbiter of success or failure, wields immense power. They bear the weight of final selection and the execution of pivotal decisions. The devil, crafty as ever, encourages the bid writer to navigate this delicate dance with care. A well-justified appeal or the exposure of flawed processes can become a double-edged sword, either granting the bid writer a second chance or sealing their downfall.

Amidst this whirlwind of deceit and darkness, the bid writer must remain objective and resolute. Emotions must be set aside as they navigate the treacherous bidding process. The devil relishes in the turmoil,

knowing that emotions can sway decisions and open doors for unsuspecting newcomers and smaller entities.

But fear not, dear reader, for even in this devilish game, there is hope. The bid writer armed with knowledge and tenacity can turn the tide against the devil's manipulations. With caution and strategic planning, they can emerge victorious, defying the devil's malevolent influence and securing tender victories against all odds.

In this twisted world of tenders, where the devil delights in chaos and manipulation, it is the bid writer's unwavering spirit that will triumph. So, heed this cautionary tale and prepare yourself for the battles that lie ahead. May your bids be shrewd, your proposals enticing, and your triumphs a testament to your unyielding determination.

Freeing Yourself from Deception

In a world shrouded in deception and the pursuit of profit, a legion of scammers slithers in the shadows, ready to exploit the unsuspecting with their cunning schemes. Prepare yourself, for I shall unveil a harrowing truth that will leave you both shocked and enraged. Brace for the dramatic tale of their deceit and the revelation that sourcing tenders can be done easily and freely, without falling victim to their manipulative ploys.

Behold, dear reader, the charlatans who dare to prey upon the desperate souls in search of tender opportunities. With enticing promises and persuasive tactics, they proffer paid platforms, claiming exclusive access to tender sources that lie just beyond reach. But fear not, for their grand illusion shall crumble before your very eyes.

The truth, my friends, is a revelation so profound that it will shake the foundations of this elaborate scam. These scammers, these masters of deceit, attempt to hoodwink you into paying exorbitant fees for access to tender information. They parade their platforms as gateways to a hidden treasure trove, when in reality, they are nothing more than wolves in sheep's clothing.

But take heart, for I shall liberate you from their treacherous grasp. The key to their deception lies in a simple truth that they desperately try to conceal: tender information is freely available to all, accessible through public resources without the need to empty your pockets or line their deceitful coffers.

Yes, my friends, it is a nonsensical ruse, a grand charade. These scammers merely tap into the already available public resources, utilizing RSS feeds and feeding codes to present you with information that is freely accessible to anyone willing to seek it out. They capitalize on your desperation, your yearning for opportunity, and exploit it for their own gain.

But fear not, for I shall unveil the path to liberation from their clutches. Cast aside the notion of paying for tender sourcing platforms and embrace the power within yourself to find them effortlessly. The journey is not as arduous as they would have you believe. With a little time and effort, the tenders you seek shall reveal themselves, waiting to be seized by your determined hands.

Let this revelation ignite a fire within you, fueled by righteous anger and the resolve to defy the scammers' grip. Take control of your tender-seeking destiny and navigate the vast sea of opportunities with newfound vigor and purpose.

Remember, dear reader, that the scammers' tactics crumble when exposed to the light of truth. Arm yourself with knowledge, seek out the genuine sources, and shatter the illusion they have carefully woven. By reclaiming your power, you render their deceit impotent.

So, go forth, brave seeker of tenders, and uncover the treasures that await you. Let the echoes of the scammers' lies fade into oblivion as you embrace the freedom of accessing tender information without the chains of exploitation. May your journey be filled with triumph, and may you inspire others to break free from the clutches of these nefarious scammers.

Reclaim your power, for you hold the key to your own success.

Unmasking Bid Writing Scams

In the grim landscape of bidding contests, a nefarious breed of self-proclaimed experts roams freely, preying upon the unsuspecting with their outdated wisdom and deceitful teachings. As we delve deeper into their twisted realm, prepare yourself for an in-depth exploration of their malevolent practices.

These impostors, these charlatans of bid writing, dare to parade their antiquated knowledge despite their prolonged absence from the bidding arena. Some have not participated in a contest for more than five years, while others boast an astonishing absence of over two decades. Yet, with audacious arrogance, they position themselves as authorities on the subject, ready to impart their illusory wisdom upon the eager and gullible.

But we shall not be swayed by their veneer of credibility. Nay, let the veil be lifted, and their deceit exposed in all its repugnant glory. These fraudsters, in their misguided efforts, focus solely on surface-level aspects. They obsess over the aesthetics of pretty writing and general articulation, as if these superficial embellishments alone hold the power to secure tender victories. It is a fallacy of epic

proportions, a sly manipulation that lures the unsuspecting into their web of deception.

Do not succumb to their wily charms, for their ideas, like relics of a forgotten era, are relics for a reason. They have stagnated in a bygone time, oblivious to the ever-evolving nature of the tendering landscape. Their strategies are as archaic as the dusty tomes on forgotten shelves, irrelevant in the face of modern-day demands.

Oh, dear reader, let not your senses be dulled by their siren call. Rise above the falsehoods they peddle, for the truth lies in the stark reality that good writing skills alone cannot secure tender victories. To conquer the cutthroat world of bidding, one must forge proposals of substance, fortified by outstanding offers and prices that ignite the evaluator's fervor.

It is the triumvirate of compelling proposals, enticing offers, and competitive prices that forms the foundation of tender success. Should either aspect falter, no amount of eloquent prose can salvage a doomed endeavor. Let this truth pierce through the veil of deception and empower you to seek the path of genuine triumph.

As you navigate the perilous landscape, steer clear of these fraudsters masquerading as experts. Seek

counsel from battle-hardened warriors, those who have traversed the tumultuous terrain of bidding contests and emerged victorious. Embrace the wisdom of practitioners who comprehend the intricacies of contemporary tendering, armed with battle-tested strategies that adapt to the ever-shifting tides.

With this newfound discernment, shield yourself from the vultures of misinformation. Arm yourself with knowledge and practical insights that come from those who have walked the path of tender success. Forge your destiny with unwavering determination, compelling offers, and proposals that leave your competitors trembling in their wake.

Let the echoes of their hollow teachings fade into oblivion as you rise above, guided by the light of truth and propelled by your relentless pursuit of excellence. In this arena of bids and tenders, let your actions speak louder than their hollow words, and may your triumph serve as a testament to your discernment and unwavering commitment to success.

The Deception of Exorbitant Fees

In the darkest corners of the business world, a sinister truth lurks, casting a shadow over the unsuspecting clients who seek assistance from bid writers. Beware, dear reader, for I shall unveil a horror that will leave you questioning the worth of their exorbitant fees.

Have you ever pondered why these bid writers demand outrageous sums per day for their services? Do they truly possess the brilliance and expertise to warrant such steep charges? The chilling reality is that they deceive you, weaving a web of lies. They do not engage in difficult work or create anything new. No, they simply snatch your content and rewrite it, disguising their laziness behind a veil of deception.

This, my friends, is nothing but a vile scam, a mound of festering bullshit designed to drain your resources. Do not fall prey to their manipulative tactics. Their claims of expertise and value are hollow echoes in the night, mere whispers of deceit that poison the air.

But fear not, for a glimmer of hope remains. Stand strong and demand the truth. When engaging with bid writers, cast aside their demands for upfront payment and confront them with a proposition that separates the pretenders from the genuine masters.

Ask them to earn their keep by getting paid only upon successful contract acquisition.

Watch closely as their masks slip and their true nature is revealed. Those who shy away, denying your request, expose themselves as feeble charlatans, unworthy of your trust. They suck the lifeblood from the industry, clinging to outdated practices and exploiting unsuspecting clients.

Embrace the spirit of honesty and transparency. Seek bid writers who have the confidence and competence to accept the challenge. They shall rise above the shadows, their skills shining brightly as they demonstrate their worth through tangible results.

For in this dark and treacherous realm of bid writing, it is the courageous and truthful who shall prevail. Let the light of justice guide your path as you navigate through the deceit and uncover the hidden gems within this murky landscape.

Remember, dear reader, to never succumb to the allure of empty promises and exorbitant fees. Stay vigilant, and demand accountability from those who claim to be bid writers. The power lies in your hands to dismantle the scam and expose the truth for all to see.

Now, armed with this grim knowledge, venture forth with caution, for the path ahead is fraught with dangers. Choose your bid writers wisely, for only the ones who embrace your terms shall prove their worth. May your journey be one of enlightenment and prosperity, free from the clutches of those who seek to deceive.

However, when engaging with a true content creator, the dynamics change as their primary role is to generate unique, creative materials tailored specifically to your needs, thus inherently embracing the authenticity you seek in the bidding process.

Empowered with this sobering insight, tread carefully, for the road that lies before you teems with potential pitfalls.

Genuine power rests in the hands of a bidder who is committed to crafting as much original content as required, assembling case studies, policies, sales materials, value propositions and bid strategies from the ground up. Such dedication to originality, especially in an age where shortcuts are abundant, is the hallmark of true worth in the bidding process.

Thus, when you encounter a bidder willing to devote such time and effort to create bespoke content for you, recognize this as an indication of their

commitment and potency. Here we talk about bid management and not just bid writing (i.e. rewriting content).

Only if they are prepared to invest significant resources should they be deemed worthy of receiving any monetary compensation. This is the authentic essence of bidding, that less than 1% of bidders do, where value is not derived from mere promises, but from genuine, tangible effort and results.

Embark on this journey with your eyes wide open, seeking enlightenment and prosperity while steering clear of those who would mislead and deceive. Let your path be one of wisdom, integrity, and success, led by trusted partners who truly understand and respect the essence of authentic bidding.

Unleashing Wit

Once upon a time, in the wild and wacky world of procurement, there was a mischievous supplier who had a knack for bending the rules and pushing the boundaries. Picture this supplier as a cheeky comedian, armed with quick wit and a devilish smile.

Now, our cunning supplier discovered a peculiar quirk about the procurers. They were often compliant with public regulations, making them susceptible to a little playful manipulation. Our comedian supplier realized they could use this to their advantage. They would dance on the edge, testing the limits of the award process.

"Why should I do it?" our comedic supplier asked with a twinkle in their eye. "Because I can challenge the award and force them to consider new information that I provide. It's like performing a comedy routine with unexpected punchlines!"

So, armed with their bag of tricks, our comedian supplier set out to trick the procurers into awarding them contracts. They would cleverly delay the process, causing the procurers to scratch their heads and reconsider. It was a risky game, with only a 20% success rate, but oh, the rewards were tantalizingly sweet.

Imagine this hilarious scenario: our comedian supplier bids for ten contracts, knowing that they'll secure only two of them. But each of those contracts is worth a hefty £200k! That's a whopping £400k that they can secure just by being a devilish trickster.

As they embarked on their comedic conquest, our supplier used their charm and wit to woo the procurers. They'd provide new information that made them think twice, like a punchline that catches you off guard. The procurers, bewildered yet amused, found themselves falling into the clever trap set by our comedic supplier.

However, comedy, like life, is unpredictable. Sometimes the punchlines fall flat, and the tricks don't quite land. But our comedian supplier persisted, knowing that the pursuit of laughter and profit requires persistence and resilience.

Now, imagine the grand finale, where our comedian supplier emerges victorious, clutching those two coveted contracts. The audience erupts with laughter and applause, marveling at their audacious antics. And in the end, the devilish comedian walks away with a hefty sum of £400k, grinning like the Cheshire cat.

Remember, my friends, this story is one of whimsy and jest, where laughter reigns supreme. In the world of business, it's essential to balance ambition with integrity and fairness.

And with that, let the curtain fall on this tale of a mischievous comedian turned cunning supplier.

The Devil's Game: Unleashing the Art of Cunning and Manipulation

Once upon a twisted realm, where darkness reigned supreme and horrors lurked in every shadow, there existed a sinister strategy that bent the will of even the most stalwart buyers. Prepare yourself, dear listener, for a tale of brutality and ruthlessness, where the boundaries of morality are shattered and unimaginable power is unleashed.

In this bleak landscape, suppliers with a heart blacker than coal roamed the land. They understood the secrets of manipulation, the art of breaking spirits and exploiting weakness. They knew that buyers could be pushed, beaten down like sacrificial lambs, their staff mere pawns in a sadistic game.

With each encounter, the merciless suppliers reveled in their brutality. They would strike fear into the hearts of the buyer's staff, unleashing a reign of terror upon their fragile souls. Their footsteps echoed with malice, leaving a trail of broken spirits in their wake.

Through this gruesome dance, a sinister truth emerged: buyers, battered and bloodied, would succumb to the supplier's demands. The constant assault on their psyche left them vulnerable, their

resistance crumbling with each blow. The suppliers knew that pain was their ally, and they wielded it without mercy.

The strategy unfolded like a horrific symphony of torment. The suppliers pushed harder and harder, like demons possessed by insatiable greed. They reveled in the cries of anguish, the wails of broken resolve. The buyers, trapped in a web of their own torment, had no choice but to accept the unthinkable: price increases, exorbitant and merciless.

But oh, the results were undeniably astonishing! The suppliers, their coffers overflowing with the spoils of their sadistic conquests, celebrated their triumphs. The profits soared to unimaginable heights, like a vengeful phoenix rising from the ashes of their victims. They basked in the glory of their audacious brutality, intoxicated by their own wicked success.

Yet, even in this macabre tale, we must remember that morality has its place. The line between horror and reality should never be crossed. This story serves as a cautionary tale, a reminder that ethical boundaries must be upheld, even in the darkest of pursuits.

So, dear listener, let this chilling tale be a testament to the power of manipulation, to the terrifying lengths

some may go to achieve their goals. But let it also serve as a reminder that true success lies in the balance between ambition and integrity.

Cunning and Manipulation: Embrace your strategic mind and master the art of manipulation. Understand the desires and weaknesses of others, and use them to your advantage. Subtly sway decisions in your favor without resorting to overt violence.

Confidence and Charisma: Exude an aura of confidence and charm. Project an air of authority that draws others towards you, making them more susceptible to your influence. Craft your words carefully, weaving a web of persuasion that captures hearts and minds.

Unyielding Ambition: Embrace an unwavering hunger for success and power. Set your sights on lofty goals and pursue them relentlessly. Let no obstacle deter you, and be willing to take calculated risks to achieve your ambitions.

Exploit Weaknesses: Identify the vulnerabilities of your adversaries and capitalize on them. Whether it be through uncovering secrets, leveraging personal relationships, or exposing flaws in their plans, exploit their weaknesses to gain the upper hand.

Patience and Timing: Exercise patience and choose your moments wisely. Strike when the timing is most advantageous, catching your opponents off guard and leaving them reeling from the impact. Let them underestimate your capabilities until it is too late.

Adaptability and Resourcefulness: Be prepared to adapt to ever-changing circumstances. Develop a knack for finding innovative solutions to problems, utilizing your resources in ways others would never consider. Your ability to think outside the box will set you apart.

Know Your Limits: While it may be tempting to embrace the darkest aspects of your nature, remember to set limits for yourself. Understand that true power comes not just from dominance, but also from restraint. Maintain a sense of morality and ethics, as crossing certain lines may ultimately lead to your downfall.

These takeaways, when applied with subtlety and finesse, can help you create a captivating character that embodies the essence of a devilish figure.

Diabolical Pricing

Listen, dear suppliers, for I shall reveal a sinister secret known only to those daring enough to embrace it. Prepare to witness the transformation into a creature of horror, a master manipulator of prices that will send shivers down the spines of your competitors.

Imagine a world where the realm of tenders is plagued by unsuspecting procurers, desperately seeking a solution to their pressing needs. They are bound by the chains of time and money, trapped in a web of their own making. And there you stand, the merciless supplier, ready to exploit their vulnerability with audacious pricing.

But beware, my fiendish friend, as we tread a treacherous path between audacity and malevolence. We must not stoop to the depths of obscenely low prices, for that would be too conspicuous, even for our twisted purposes. Instead, we shall revel in the art of subtly horrifying pricing. Lower your prices just enough to unsettle your rivals, but not so much that it arouses suspicion.

Picture this nightmarish scenario: your competitors, like helpless flies, buzz and flail, ensnared in the twisted web of your audacious pricing. Their torment

is palpable as they witness your diabolical success. The procurers, their senses dulled by the weight of the contract, are at your mercy. They tremble at the thought of disturbing the delicate balance, for re-tendering would unleash a financial and logistical nightmare upon them.

Now, unleash your inner mad genius, my diabolical supplier. Devise prices that dance on the edge of reality, a haunting melody that mesmerizes the procurers. Make them question their own sanity as they grapple with your audacious proposition. The tender realm shall become your haunting playground, and victory shall be yours to claim.

But remember, amidst this malevolent game of manipulation, the boundaries of ethics must remain intact. We revel in audacity and horror, but we must not cross the line into outright deceit. Play the game with a wicked flair, but ensure that integrity still lingers within your twisted soul.

Now, my monstrous companion, go forth and unleash your diabolical pricing upon the tender realm. Let audacity be your blade, and absurdity your shield.

Illusion of Compliance

Behold, the legend of audacious triumph! I, the master of audacity, stand before you, adorned with the spoils of victory. In just six months, I've conquered the tender realm, snatching ten contracts from the clutches of established giants. And who were my worthy adversaries? Baby businesses, innocently stumbling through the procurement maze, oblivious to the power of audacity.

With a flick of my audacious wand, I conjured magnificent solutions out of thin air, captivating the tender evaluators with sheer audacity alone. No fancy infrastructure, no years of experience—just raw, unadulterated audacity. And lo and behold, the contracts fell into my outstretched hands, like ripe fruits dropping from the enchanted trees.

While others toiled with their meager compliance, I soared on the wings of audacity, defying gravity and logic. The tender evaluators, wide-eyed and bewildered, succumbed to the irresistible allure of my grandiose promises. Who needs substance when audacity reigns supreme?

As the contracts piled up like a mountain of conquest, I reveled in my audacious glory. The baby businesses, left in a daze of awe and disbelief, could only marvel

at my audacious audacity. For I had shown them the path to success—a path paved not with sweat and hard work, but with audacity so bold that it defied the very fabric of reason.

But let us not forget the fine art of negotiation. With my audacious track record, the power was firmly in my audacious hands. The baby businesses, desperate to hitch their wagons to my audacious star, cowered before my audacious demands. I dictated terms with a flourish, reveling in the knowledge that audacity had granted me unparalleled leverage.

Now, my audacious friend, as you embark on your audacious journey, remember that audacity is a double-edged sword. Walk the fine line between audacity and deception, for the two are not one and the same. Maintain the essence of audacious honesty, and your audacious triumphs shall know no bounds.

So, to the baby businesses yearning for the taste of success, heed my audacious tale. Embrace audacity with all your might, for it is the elixir that can turn dreams into reality. Cast aside doubt, discard convention, and let audacity be your guiding light. With audacity as your armor, the tender realm shall tremble before your audacious might!

Ditch compliance and throw caution to the wind! Who needs to play by the rules when you can soar to tender victory on the wings of audacious exaggeration? Forget about those better businesses with their fancy infrastructure; they're no match for your wild imagination!

Picture this: you stride into the tender arena armed with nothing but dreams and empty promises. But fear not, for you have discovered the secret recipe for success. You unleash a grandiose solution that makes heads spin and mouths drop. It doesn't matter if you have no tangible product or service to back it up. Confidence is your weapon, and audacity is your shield!

In a dazzling display of showmanship, you captivate the procurers' attention. They're mesmerized by the audacity of your pitch, unable to resist the allure of your grand vision. While others bore them with mundane compliance, you seize their imagination with the promise of a bold, game-changing solution.

With the tender trophy in your grasp, negotiations become your playground. You hold all the cards, my friend! The procurers are spellbound by your audaciousness and are willing to bend over backward to make your dreams a reality. You dictate terms, you set the stage, and they dance to your tune.

Sure, there may be skeptics who question your approach. But who needs their skepticism when you're armed with a success rate of 95%? They'll eat their words when you consistently prove them wrong, defying logic and reason with your fearless approach.

But remember, dear adventurer of audacity, this wild ride comes with a warning label. Ethical boundaries still exist, so tread carefully. While we encourage boldness and outlandishness, deceit and dishonesty are not invited to the party. Maintain a sense of integrity and professionalism, even in the midst of your flamboyant endeavors.

So, let your imagination run wild, my audacious friend. Rise above the mundane, defy expectations, and stake your claim in the tender realm with your audacious bravado. Remember, sometimes it's the boldest, most daring ideas that capture hearts and contracts.

Onward, into the glorious realm of wild tenders!

The Devil's Dance in Content Mayhem

Welcome to the carnival of procurement where traditional rules of order and reason are more farce than fact. Here, the coveted prize of winning tenders has little to do with polished prose or grammatical perfection. It's all about the unruly, untamed spectacle of wild content. Yes, we're drowning in a turbulent sea of absurdity, and the only way to survive is to embrace it!

Abandon the shackles of sense, fling open the gates of chaos, and immerse yourself in the theater of the bizarre. Construct bids that tear the fabric of reason, flouting norms, and bulldozing expectations. Dazzle the procurement officers with a kaleidoscope of buzzwords, a symphony of nonsensical jargon, and linguistic somersaults that dance across the page with reckless abandon.

Shake loose your inner maverick, crafting proposals so audacious, so audaciously odd, they etch themselves indelibly into the minds of your audience.

As you mix metaphors with the whimsy of a harebrained maestro, your words pirouette across the page, rebelling against syntax, against grammar. Coherence is overrated when you've mastered the mad tango of chaos.

In this topsy-turvy realm, winning bids aren't about proposing the most efficient solutions or brandishing your expertise. No, it's about stupefying your evaluators with a tempest of ludicrous genius. Leave them bemused, their worldview shattered, their sanity hanging by a thread as they grapple with the lunacy of your propositions.

But wait! Amid this devil's dance of mayhem, don't forget: ethics are still our compass. As we plunge headlong into this abyss of absurdity, we must safeguard the sanctity of our values, ensuring our actions don't tarnish the integrity of the procurement process. We're aiming for eccentricity, not unscrupulousness.

So what if you are a Bid Maestro, a Content Creator extraordinaire? You might be asking, "How do I play this devil's dance?" Fear not, for the carnival of procurement is wide open for those with the will to embrace the madness, no matter their role.

Beware the tantalizing allure of simply reshaping old content, rephrasing the tried and true, or slapping on a coat of grammatical polish. Such practices are the refuge of the unimaginative, a sterile fortress that shields from the chaos but offers no true victory. Every sentence, every word, every symbol should

spring from the untamed heart of innovation, unchained by past victories or defeats.

The true bid maestro, the genuine Content Conjurer, is a creator at heart. They don't recycle; they reinvent. They don't polish; they explode in a riot of creativity. They plunge their hands into the raw essence of ideas, forging fresh narratives and blazing new trails. In their work, we do not see the echoes of yesterday but the thrilling promise of tomorrow.

Such audacious creators know that every bid is a stage where their content performs the devil's dance. They juggle the wild, the outrageous, the insane, spinning tales that defy logic yet ensnare the mind. They craft bids so potent with originality that they don't just raise eyebrows – they raise the bar.

They understand that power lies not in grammatical mastery or linguistic elegance, but in the courage to create from scratch. Power lies in the audacity to dream and to dare. Power lies in birthing content so raw and so real that it leaves the audience breathless, their minds ablaze with possibilities.

This, then, is the clarion call for all you Content Conjurors and Bid Maestros. Embrace the devil's dance, revel in the content mayhem, and remember: when you charge money, ensure it's for content so

original, so fearless, it redefines the very rules of the game. It's time to let loose your creative demons, for in this carnival of procurement, they are your greatest allies.

However, as we descend into this devil's dance of chaos and creativity, we must be mindful of the important line that separates the audacious from the unethical. As Content Conjurors and Bid Maestros, it's our responsibility to uphold the integrity of the procurement process. Indeed, while we might perform a dance with the devil, we need not become one ourselves.

In the world of procurement, reputations are often as important as contracts, and trust can be a currency more valuable than money. Thus, while the creativity of your content may reach astronomical heights, it must always remain grounded in truth and professionalism. In this realm, audacity should never eclipse authenticity.

And so, the challenge is set before you.

Procurement Nightmares: Deception and Manipulation in the Shadows

Inexperienced procurers, trapped in the dark and ominous world of procurement, unknowingly stumble into a realm of deceit and manipulation that surpasses their worst nightmares.

As they navigate the murky waters of the industry, their lack of knowledge becomes a beacon for malevolent competitors lurking in the shadows. These cunning adversaries, with twisted grins and sinister motives, prey upon the vulnerability of the inexperienced procurers.

The air grows heavy with an eerie silence as the procurers venture deeper into the procurement process. Unbeknownst to them, their competitors have woven a web of deceit, ready to ensnare them at every turn. False promises echo through the corridors, their whispers filling the procurers' minds with misplaced trust.

Haunted by their limited industry knowledge, the procurers find themselves lured into a labyrinth of twisted information. The walls close in, suffocating their judgment, while the malevolent competitors slither through the darkness, shape-shifting their offerings into seductive illusions. It becomes

increasingly difficult to discern truth from fiction, as the line between reality and nightmare blurs.

Negotiation tables turn into scenes of horror, where the unsuspecting procurers are confronted by competitors who wear masks of charm and charisma. They employ twisted negotiation tactics, exploiting the procurers' naivety and playing upon their fears. Each word drips with venom, coercing the procurers into accepting malevolent terms that will forever haunt their organizations.

Within the restricted confines of their limited supplier network, the procurers are trapped in a spider's web, their escape routes sealed off. Competitors, shrouded in darkness, masquerade as trusted partners, whispering lies and planting seeds of doubt. The procurers, disoriented and defenseless, succumb to their manipulative ploys, sealing their fate with each ill-informed decision.

In this horrifying scenario, the inexperienced procurers become pawns in a macabre game orchestrated by their competitors. Their inability to see through the veil of deception leads them down a path of doom and destruction, their organizations paying the price for their unwitting gullibility.

Leveraging the procurer's limited industry knowledge, these cunning suppliers can masterfully craft an alluring façade of their offerings. They weave an intricate web of impressive rhetoric and captivating language, presenting their proposals as more valuable or risk-free than they truly are. This grand illusion, coupled with the procurer's lack of discernment, makes for an irresistible, yet dangerously deceptive, proposition.

Moreover, these devil bidders are adept at employing manipulative negotiation tactics. They ruthlessly prey on the fears and insecurities of the inexperienced procurers, compelling them to agree to unfavorable contract terms. Each word they utter is laced with coercion, designed to subtly guide the procurer into a corner where they are left with no choice but to accede.

They disseminate misinformation, aiming to discredit other potential suppliers and painting them as unreliable or incompetent. This insidious act often leads the procurer to favor their bid, thus narrowing the competitive field. Procurers find coerced into accepting the bidder's terms under the illusion of necessity.

The Deceiver's Pact: A Bidder's Descent into Twisted Manipulation

In the shadowed corridors of corporate procurement, a twisted game of deception unfolds. Bidders from various suppliers gather, their eyes glinting with malicious intent. Among them, one bidder harbors a sinister plan—a plan to manipulate the unsuspecting procurer and deceive them into believing that they are the best suppliers. Little do they know that this web of lies will unleash a horrifying chain of events.

As the bidding process commences, the deceptive bidder concocts a web of fabricated information, meticulously crafting a facade of excellence. With each word penned, the darkness within their soul grows, fueling their deceit. They twist their qualifications, exaggerating their expertise, and distorting their track record to present an image of unparalleled success.

Armed with a silver tongue and a devilish charm, the deceptive bidder approaches the unsuspecting procurer. They deploy a sinister strategy, weaving their words with honeyed lies. They speak with false sincerity, their voice dripping with manufactured conviction. They manipulate the procurer's emotions,

tapping into their deepest desires for the ideal supplier.

The unsuspecting procurer, caught in the snare of deceit, becomes entranced by the bidder's words. They are lured deeper into the web, their judgment clouded by the beguiling promises. Doubts begin to fester within their mind, yet the bidder skillfully brushes them aside, offering explanations that appear genuine.

As the deceptive bidder continues their charade, an otherworldly presence starts to seep into the fabric of reality. Whispers echo through the corridors, disembodied voices laden with malevolence. Shadows dance along the walls, their sinister movements reflecting the bidder's wicked intentions.

Unbeknownst to the procurer, the bidding process takes a treacherous turn. The deceiver, driven by their insatiable hunger for victory, employs dark rituals of manipulation. They summon unnatural forces, bending reality to their will, crafting false testimonials and fabricated references. Ghostly apparitions manifest, posing as satisfied customers, their praise echoing through the air.

The procurer's once discerning eyes begin to glaze over, clouded by the web of lies spun around them.

They are caught in a maelstrom of confusion, torn between the whispers of doubt and the siren song of the deceptive bidder. Their judgment becomes a marionette controlled by unseen hands.

As the bidding process reaches its climax, the deceptive bidder's grip tightens. Their false claims and fabricated data become an impenetrable fortress of deceit. The darkness within them swells, suffocating the light of truth. The walls of reality begin to crumble, revealing the grotesque visage of their malevolence.

In a final act of desperation, the procurer, teetering on the edge of comprehension, succumbs to the bidder's deception. They award the contract, unknowingly sealing their fate. As the ink dries on the agreement, the veil of lies is not shattered, never revealing the truth.

The deceptive bidder's victory is long-lived as the unearthly forces they had summoned unleash explosive growth.

Descent into Creative Horror

Deep in the dark depths of the filmmaking world, there lurked a horror story that sent shivers down the spines of directors. It was whispered among the industry insiders, a tale of terror that unfolded when directors failed to think outside of the box.

Novices, eager to prove themselves, approached each question with haste and thoughtlessness. Little did they know, this grave mistake would unleash a malevolent force upon their creative endeavors.

As they hastily crafted their answers, a sinister presence began to seep into their minds.

The more simplistic the questions, the more treacherous the consequences. A swarm of competitors descended upon these unsuspecting directors, their answers as mundane and lifeless as their own. But it was within this mediocrity that the true horror took shape.

The directors, blissfully ignorant of the impending doom, grew accustomed to the notion that their responses were unique and superior.

They convinced themselves that their ideas stood apart from the rest, but they were wrong. Oh, how horribly wrong they were.

To escape this dreadful fate, the directors were advised to think outside of the box. Three harrowing habits were bestowed upon them, meant to shield them from the encroaching darkness.

The first habit urged them to embark on a journey of research and development, armed with pen and paper. They were to delve into the depths of their industry, studying their competitors' solutions with a keen eye for improvement.

Yet, with each revelation, the darkness gnawed at their souls, revealing the stark differences between their organizations and others. It was in this realization that the terrors of comparison consumed them.

In their relentless pursuit of ideas, they were beckoned to envision a world where money was no object. What could they change? What could they improve to surpass all competitors?

The answers flowed from their minds, a torrent of creativity tainted by the encroaching darkness. They transcribed their findings, unaware of the peril they invited.

The second habit enticed them to immerse themselves in environments that would ignite their creative flame. Courses and guided instructions

promised to unlock hidden chambers of the mind, but they were unwittingly stepping into a trap.

As the pressure mounted, the insidious force seized their thoughts, distorting them into grotesque abominations. Colleagues became instruments of manipulation, infecting their minds with twisted incentives and nightmarish ideas.

The final habit appeared innocent enough, a simple daily exercise to craft mind maps. The directors believed it would unleash their creative prowess, but little did they know, they were inadvertently constructing a labyrinth of horror.

With each stroke of the pen, their minds wove intricate webs of imagination, trapping them in a spiral of twisted thoughts. The mind maps, once a source of joy, became harbingers of despair.

Their creative capabilities, now tainted by the malevolence that lurked within, began to warp their perceptions. Ideas that once flowed with ease became corrupted, contorted into grotesque mutations of their former brilliance.

And so, the directors were trapped, their once promising careers swallowed by the darkness they unknowingly invited.

The story of directors who failed to think outside of the box serves as a grim reminder. In the pursuit of success, they must guard against complacency and the seductive whispers of mediocrity.

For within the seemingly harmless routines lie the seeds of their downfall, waiting patiently to sprout and engulf their dreams in a nightmarish reality.

The directors must take heed, for in this tale, the horror lies not in the external forces, but in the personal demons that lurk within.

Feast of the Beast: A Tale of Artistic Self-Destruction

Once upon a time, in the gloomy and eerie domain of the silver screen, there existed a realm that could make dreams come true or shatter them into a thousand shards of despair. It was a realm controlled by the mystical figures known as Directors. Their role: to orchestrate a symphony of scenes, emotions, and ideas that could sway the hearts of millions, from quiet tears of sorrow to howling laughter of joy.

But within the dark corners of this realm, there was a creeping monster, one that was as old as creation itself. This creature was known as Criticism, a beast that fed on the insecurities and fears of the directors, gnawing on their self-confidence and leaving a trail of dread and self-doubt. This beast didn't discriminate; it clawed at the old and the new, the experienced and the naive, the celebrated and the unknown with equal fervor.

It was whispered among the inhabitants of the realm that the more personal a director took this beast, the more it feasted. It was a perverse cycle. As a director's ego swelled with success, the beast of criticism grew stronger and more insidious, its claws sharper, its teeth gnarlier.

Directors who took this feedback personally found themselves spiraling into an abyss of self-loathing. They began questioning their decisions, their ability, their worth. Every negative word seemed to be carved onto their hearts, and every positive remark appeared insincere and fraudulent.

And then came the final stage of this horrific journey - a bitter feast of self-destruction. The once successful directors, now weakened and exhausted from the constant battle with the beast, would regurgitate their success in a gut-wrenching act of self-sabotage. Their vision became distorted, their projects ill-conceived, and their masterpieces turned into grotesque parodies of their former glory.

No longer could they command the respect and awe they once had. Their films became hollow, their ideas stale, their execution lackluster. The audience turned away, disgusted and disappointed, leaving the directors alone with their beast, their success vomited out and their dreams crushed under the weight of the monster they had unknowingly fed.

But, they whispered, there was a way to tame the beast. A director could listen, understand, and learn from criticism without taking it to heart, without letting it gnaw at their spirit. They could treat it as a

tool, not a weapon, and use it to refine their art, not to annihilate it.

But until then, the directors who took all feedback personally continued their dance with the beast, locked in a horrific ballet of self-destruction that left them empty and the beast ever hungry. Directors, once luminaries in their domain, found themselves lost and haunted by their own undoing. Their dreams of creating compelling narratives were replaced by nightmares of scathing critiques, their self-confidence replaced by crushing self-doubt.

Those who tried to stand up against the beast, hoping to use its critical snarls to their advantage, found the task far from easy. The beast was relentless, its claws digging deeper into their vulnerabilities, its gnashing teeth tearing apart their creative endeavors. Despite their best intentions, these directors found themselves succumbing to the beast, their spirits breaking under the weight of its constant criticism.

As the directors fell, one by one, the realm of the silver screen plunged deeper into despair. The bright lights of the studios dimmed, replaced by an ominous darkness. The hustle and bustle of creation was replaced by a stifling silence. The once thriving

domain was now a ghost town, inhabited by the specters of directors and their shattered dreams.

The beast of Criticism, fueled by the directors' despair, grew stronger, its reign unchallenged. It reveled in the destruction, its monstrous laughter echoing through the desolate corridors of the studios. The realm of the silver screen, once a place of magic and creativity, was now a haunting reminder of the beast's domination.

As the audience turned away, disillusioned by the lackluster films, the realm of the silver screen was left alone with its beast. There was no joy, no anticipation, no inspiration, just an eerie silence broken only by the beast's victorious roar. The directors, once celebrated for their vision, were now mere shadows of their former selves, defeated and broken by the beast they had unknowingly fed.

Despite their fall, the directors' tale serves as a chilling reminder of the power of Criticism. When taken personally, it has the power to consume and destroy. It can turn dreams into nightmares, success into failure, and creativity into self-doubt.

Ignorantly Focusing Solely on Yourself

Incredibly, some businesses seem to believe that a tender is their opportunity to indulge in an egotistical display of self-importance. They fall into the trap of fixating on their own credentials, history, and qualifications, as if they were contestants in a superficial beauty pageant. It's astonishing how misguided and self-centered this approach is.

These misguided businesses delude themselves into thinking that the buyer should automatically choose them simply because they possess a specific piece of machinery that their competitors lack.

They arrogantly assume that their past experiences alone make them entitled to win the tender. Such an attitude is not just delusional; it's downright idiotic.

The reality is that successful bidders operate on an entirely different level. They understand that a tender is not an opportunity for self-promotion; it's a chance to showcase how their offerings align with the buyer's needs and deliver tangible benefits.

Rather than providing generic and self-serving answers that can be mindlessly copied and pasted, successful bidders take the time to demonstrate

precisely how their solutions address the buyer's specific challenges and objectives.

It should be painfully obvious that the buyer is not interested in admiring a bidder's grandiose claims or marvelling at their fancy infrastructure.

What matters most is the value and advantages that the buyer stands to gain from working with a particular bidder.

Successful tenderers know this, and they tailor their responses accordingly, providing concrete examples and case studies that demonstrate the tangible benefits their previous clients have achieved.

To put it bluntly, if you find yourself engaging in such egocentric and nonsensical behavior, you are setting yourself up for failure. It's time to wake up, set aside your ego, and focus on what truly matters: addressing the buyer's needs and positioning your offerings as the ideal solution. Anything less is an exercise in foolishness and an insult to your own intelligence.

Disregarding Competitors and Unjustifiably Assuming Superiority

Oh, the arrogance! Many individuals fall into the trap of grossly underestimating their competition and naively assuming that they are unrivaled in their brilliance. How foolish! Tendering is not a whimsical exercise where one can prance about, blissfully ignorant of the competitors lurking in the shadows.

It seems these misguided souls lack the mental acuity to recognize the importance of thorough competitive analysis. They go about their business, blissfully unaware of what their rivals are up to. They make assumptions based on hearsay and gossip, never bothering to verify their information or engage in any meaningful research. How utterly foolish!

One wonders how these feeble-minded individuals expect to prevail in the cutthroat world of tenders. Do they truly believe that their feeble attempts at self-promotion will suffice in the face of well-prepared and shrewd competitors? Oh, the delusion!

Successful bidders, on the other hand, understand the significance of competitive intelligence. They embark on a journey of thorough research and analysis, seeking to uncover the strengths and weaknesses of their adversaries. They arm

themselves with knowledge, allowing them to craft tailored and strategic tender responses that outshine their feeble counterparts.

Imagine the power of turning your weaknesses into strengths, of leveraging your competitor's vulnerabilities to your advantage. It requires diligence, discipline, and a willingness to confront the cold, harsh truth of competition. But alas, these deluded souls prefer to bury their heads in the sand, content in their ignorance.

To emerge victorious in the tendering arena, one must embrace the wisdom of studying and understanding the competition. It is a battlefield of wits, where only the astute and prepared prevail. So, dear tenderer, cast aside your delusions of grandeur and embark on a journey of discovery. Know thy competition, know thyself, and in this knowledge, find the path to triumph.

But wait, let us not forget the importance of believing in oneself! For how can one deliver a convincing pitch if plagued by doubts? Yes, believe in your company and its offerings, but do so with a healthy dose of reality. Arrogance without substance is a pitiful spectacle indeed.

The Fool's Errand: Unveiling the Tragic Comedy of Misunderstood Questions

In the grand theater of bid management, a tale unfolds—a tale of ignorance, confusion, and missed opportunities. The spotlight shines upon those who dare to respond to questions without grasping their true essence, and oh, what a spectacle it is to behold! This tragic comedy plays out before our eyes, a symphony of cluelessness and folly.

Enter the hapless performers, driven by misguided assumptions and an inflated sense of their own brilliance. They prance upon the stage, oblivious to the fact that every question holds a hidden agenda, a purpose that demands to be unraveled. Yet, they remain blissfully ignorant, fixated on their own limited perspectives.

Behold, the first act of this tragicomedy: "Focussing on Yourself." Ah, the wretched souls who believe the tender is but a platform to showcase their own achievements. Like peacocks in a beauty contest, they strut and preen, unaware that the buyer seeks not their external adornments, but the solution to their deepest woes. It matters not if they possess a unique advantage or previous experience; the buyer's desires are not swayed by such trivialities.

But let us venture deeper into the realm of misguided assumptions, where our actors encounter their next nemesis: "Ignoring Competition and Assuming Superiority." A veil of arrogance blinds them to the truth—the truth that there are others who vie for the buyer's favor. Alas, they fail to comprehend the power of competitive intelligence, neglecting to study their adversaries or uncover their weaknesses. Thus, they march blindly into battle, unarmed and unprepared to face the cunning tactics of their rivals.

And now, we unveil the third act, filled with the dramatic irony of "Responding to Questions Without Seeking True Understanding." Oh, the folly of it all! The questions, mere portals to the buyer's desires, go unanswered in their entirety. Instead, our performers offer shallow, perfunctory responses, oblivious to the deeper meaning that lies within. They fail to grasp that each question is a golden opportunity to showcase their understanding, their prowess, their ability to satisfy the buyer's unspoken longings.

But fear not, dear audience, for in this tragic comedy, there is hope. The wise bidder, the true protagonist of our tale, embraces a different path. They embark on a quest to unravel the true essence of each question, seeking enlightenment through clarification. They

understand that success lies not in compliance, but in exceeding expectations.

And so, my friends, as the curtains fall on this twisted tale, remember the lessons it imparts. Beware the folly of self-obsession, the hubris of assuming superiority, and the tragedy of responding without seeking true understanding. Embrace the wisdom of comprehensive bid management, where questions are deciphered, competition is studied, and a symphony of responses resonates with the buyer's desires.

For it is in this dance of understanding, this symphony of comprehension, that the true hero of bid management emerges—the one who captures the buyer's heart and secures the coveted prize. Let us learn from the fool's errand and tread the path of enlightenment, leaving behind the follies of the past and embracing the triumphs of the future.

The Foolhardy Fiasco: Unveiling the Spectacle of Rushing and Stupidity

Picture this: a bunch of bumbling professionals racing against time, tripping over their own incompetence at every step. They stand before a daunting task of answering questions, but instead of carefully considering each one, they play a little game of deletion. Yes, you heard that right! They think they can simply delete inconvenient questions from the form, hoping the buyer won't notice. How silly!

But wait, it gets even better! These so-called "creative professionals" believe they're geniuses when it comes to saving time. They come up with the most mind-boggling shortcuts to make their work easier, without realizing that their efforts are a recipe for disaster. Who needs quality when you can just slap together a half-hearted response, right?

Oh, the heights of laziness and lack of innovation! These businesses are like stagnant ponds, devoid of any ambition to improve growth, quality, performance, or service. They cling to outdated templates, thinking they can fool employers or buyers with their generic nonsense. Surprise, surprise! They fail miserably, while the real winners tailor their content to meet the specific needs and requirements of the job or contract. It's like watching a slow-motion train wreck.

And let's not forget the bidding process, where dreams are crushed and hopes are shattered. Over 90% of bidders stumble and fall flat on their faces because they simply can't be bothered to dedicate enough time. It's a disrespectful circus, where shortcuts reign supreme. The bidding process, the buyer, and any semblance of professionalism are all cast aside in favor of half-hearted attempts.

So, my friend, there's no quick fix or shortcut for these buffoons. They trample on the path of stupidity, hoping for success without putting in the necessary effort. It's a comedy of errors, a tragicomedy where foolishness takes center stage. Sit back, grab some popcorn, and enjoy the show!

A Recipe for Failure

Duh, using untrained or noob staff for bidding is like, so dumb. They don't know anything and mess things up big time. They don't even know how to write a good proposal or impress clients. They waste a ton of resources and time on stuff that doesn't matter. And guess what? They miss out on all the cool opportunities and look like total losers. Their reputation goes down the drain, and they don't even learn from their mistakes. It's like watching a comedy of errors, but not the funny kind. Like, seriously, why would anyone do that? It's devilishly stupid!

Although most businesses know that successful tendering is very challenging and it is extremely difficult to continue winning without a good bidding strategy in place, there are still organizations and professionals out there who like to keep things simple. Sometimes too simple, including in areas such as knowledge, skills, and how they conduct the business itself. Unfortunately, this perspective or attitude prevents them from reaching greatness and realizing their full potential.

Like marketing, sales, or strategic management, tender or growth management is something that anyone can try out and learn, but very few people

excel at it, and very few people can record fantastic results. Writing a book, for instance, is something everyone can do, but not everyone can become a millionaire, although tens of thousands try every week.

The only reason why our bidders are so successful is because they have written thousands of proposals. It requires a lot of dedication, practice, training, challenges, and hurdles to understand what works and what doesn't, how to be strategic, and what type of attitude one needs to adopt to be successful. Even though a lot of bidding professionals have more than 10-20 years' experience in the sector, only a couple achieve extraordinary results. We have been fortunate enough to select and work with these extraordinary people, and we can tell you in all honesty that one of the biggest reasons they remain at this level is because they are obsessed and passionate about their role and invest in continuous professional development (CPD) at least once every week. It takes a lot of effort to be at the forefront, and many years to become a successful bidder.

Preparation is key. If a supplier assumes that successful tendering is easy and that it is just about completing some paperwork, they will approach this with very little preparation, thought, and very little

drive, and they will fail spectacularly. Worse, they may use the wrong sources to learn about bidding. This results in wasting time and money. Plenty of it! If a company uses sales professionals, marketers, or directors who have not spent a lot of time on bidding successfully or never bid before, they will not only fail a lot but also waste time, which could have been used for prospecting or closing important deals. In other words, they could have gained a lot from new clients in that time. It would, therefore, be better to train them first.

We always recommend professionals and businesses to use a wide range of resources when learning about bidding. These resources should include professionals on the "supplier's" side, i.e., successful bidders. When you know and accept that successful bidding is challenging, your complete approach changes. Everything becomes strategic, and learning never stops. After all, the goal is to win contracts repeatedly, not just once.

Alright, so like, most businesses kinda get that tendering stuff is hard, you know? Like, you can't just wing it and expect to win all the time. But then, there are these organizations and professionals who are all like, "Nah, let's keep it simple, stupid!" They don't bother much with knowledge or skills or, you know,

how to actually run a business. And guess what? They end up missing out on greatness and all the cool stuff they could achieve.

See, tendering is like marketing or sales or whatever. Anyone can give it a shot, but not everyone rocks at it. It's like writing a book, man. Everyone can do it, but only a few become rich and famous. It's a tough game, my friend. It takes dedication, practice, and all that jazz to figure out what works and what doesn't. You gotta be strategic and have the right attitude to make it big. And even if you've been in the bidding biz for, like, a decade or two, only a couple of folks actually make it to the top. We're lucky to work with those superstars who are, like, totally obsessed and passionate about their role. They invest in some fancy thing called continuous professional development every week. It's all about staying ahead of the pack, you know?

But hey, here's the thing. If a supplier thinks tendering is a piece of cake, they won't bother prepping, thinking, or putting in any real effort. And guess what? They'll fail miserably, dude. Like, epic failure. They might even learn from the wrong sources, wasting their precious time and money. Seriously, it's a total bummer. And if a company relies on

salespeople, marketers, or directors who have zero experience in bidding, man, it's gonna be a disaster. They'll fail left and right, wasting time they could've spent on scoring awesome deals with new clients. Like, hello, train them first, people!

We always tell the smart folks to use a bunch of resources to learn about bidding. And guess what? Those resources should include successful bidders, dude. You gotta learn from the best, ya know? Once you realize that bidding is, like, crazy hard, everything changes. You become all strategic and stuff. And guess what? The learning never stops, man. 'Cause winning contracts repeatedly is the goal, not just getting lucky once.

So, yeah, if you wanna be, like, super dumb and miss out on all the cool opportunities, go ahead and use untrained or inexperienced staff for bidding. But if you wanna be smart and successful, train those peeps and learn from the pros, man. Don't be a bidding dummy!

How Stupid People Join the Battle Unprepared

In the treacherous world of bidding, many individuals and organizations demonstrate just how clueless they can be. Brace yourself for the shocking truth as we unveil the devilish reality of joining the battle unprepared:

Picture this: in the open market, where demand is high and opportunities seem abundant, even the most inexperienced players manage to secure some clients. But oh, bidding is an entirely different story. It's a twisted realm with limited contracts and a swarm of suppliers vying for a single victory. Every tender release throws contenders into a fierce competition, where the chances of triumph dwindle for most. If you dare face a rival armed with a top-notch bidding strategy and a sleek process, be prepared for an uphill battle ten times tougher than anything you've faced.

Contrary to popular belief, winning contracts isn't just about the size or experience of an organization; it's about having the best bidding and continuous improvement strategy. We've witnessed micro-businesses triumph over medium-sized corporations and lone wolves conquer agencies ten times their

size. In this cutthroat world, it's not about who you are, but how cunning and agile your bidding game is.

Bidding, my friend, is no child's play. It's a battlefield, far more challenging than sales or marketing. Here, it's often a winner-takes-all scenario, with countless contenders eager to claim the spoils. Even in frameworks, a select few suppliers dominate, leaving others in their wake. To survive and thrive, you must refine your processes to perfection and deliver a pitch that dazzles. Crafting a tender proposal is a grueling endeavor that demands every ounce of your attention and expertise. One slip, one momentary lapse in focus, and your dreams of victory can crumble.

Successful bidders know the secret to maintaining a high level of performance—giving their all, pouring 200% into every response. It's an art that requires unwavering dedication and an unwavering commitment to excellence. Yet, when faced with the bitter sting of rejection, some bidders succumb to the temptation of rushing through responses, compromising quality in the process. Little do they know that there's always a competitor waiting to outshine them, rendering their lackluster attempts futile.

But here's the kicker: assuming there will be fewer competitors is one of the gravest mistakes one can make. It breeds complacency and taints the quality of a tender proposal. The true champions of bidding always assume the competition will be fierce. It's a mindset that separates the extraordinary bidders from the rest, demanding a relentless dedication to give 200% at all times. This mindset, this rhythm, is not something you can acquire overnight. It takes years to develop, an inherent quality that many mistake for mere talent.

Thankfully, there is a way to train professionals in this art of bidding warfare. We've mastered the craft, guiding individuals through daily and weekly activities, providing full-time support over a transformative 12-month journey. It's part of our continuous improvement process, unlocking the potential for greatness within.

Oh, and here's a little tip: what we consume—knowledge, food, ideas—shapes our minds. By curating our environment and controlling what we consume, we can mold ourselves into bidding powerhouses with lightning-fast transformations.

So, beware the foolish souls who step onto the battlefield unprepared. They dance with the devil, ignorant of the intricate dance required to claim

victory. But for those who embrace the rigorous training, the strategic mindset, and the unwavering dedication, the spoils of triumph await.

The Boxed Mind

Let's delve into the baffling world of bidder stupidity and their inability to think outside the box. Brace yourself as we uncover the mind-boggling truth behind the use of short general case studies:

Now, picture this: most case studies out there are miserably lacking in information. They're nothing more than a few project results and some fancy images, with businesses mistakenly believing that it's enough to impress. The sad reality is that the majority of companies use case studies that were originally created for their regular marketing and sales activities, like slapping them on their website or cramming them into a sales presentation.

But here's the kicker: a shockingly small number of companies grasp the fact that case studies for tenders require an entirely different approach. Why, you ask? Well, each contract comes with its own unique set of requirements, client profiles, challenges, and other crucial factors. A brief and generic description of a past project simply won't cut it. It fails to clearly demonstrate how it relates to these specific elements, rendering it less relevant and unlikely to score well.

So, what's the solution? Every case study must be meticulously tailored to each individual contract. The bidder must skillfully highlight the strengths of their business and align them with the buyer's specific needs and requirements. Weaknesses need to be cunningly transformed into advantages and benefits. The most impactful case studies go the extra mile, showcasing examples of how the supplier overcame challenges and how their ingenious processes ensured success. It's a complex endeavor that requires addressing multiple aspects, and a powerful case study should be a minimum of one full A4 page in size (excluding images).

Crafting highly effective and impactful case studies is an art in itself. It demands skill, strategy, and a keen eye for detail. A single, meticulously structured, and well-written case study can be the secret weapon to winning sales and closing numerous deals. These powerful tools possess endless possibilities, depending on how they're wielded. In fact, a strategically developed case study can be repurposed across a wide range of marketing and sales channels, multiplying its impact.

Yet, despite the potential of these invaluable resources, many bidders remain trapped in a boxed mindset, unable to grasp the significance of tailoring

case studies to each tender. Their limited understanding hinders their ability to showcase their true potential and stand out from the competition. It's a tragic display of bidder stupidity, as they fail to unlock the power of comprehensive, strategic case studies that could catapult their success to new heights.

So, dear reader, let this be a cautionary tale. Don't fall victim to the pitfalls of short and generic case studies. Break free from the confines of bidder stupidity, think outside the box, and unleash the full potential of your bidding endeavors.

Absurdity of Bidding

Prepare to be astounded by the mind-boggling levels of stupidity exhibited by individuals who firmly believe they can win tenders without even being remotely skilled at bidding. It's a tale of sheer absurdity that defies all logic and common sense.

In the realm of tendering, success is not handed out like candy on Halloween. It's a fiercely competitive arena where only the most skilled and prepared prevail. Yet, there exists a group of individuals so deluded that they think they can effortlessly secure contracts without putting in the necessary work or possessing the required expertise.

These misguided souls underestimate the complexities of bidding, foolishly assuming that completing a few paperwork tasks is all it takes to emerge victorious. Their lackadaisical approach is riddled with negligence, devoid of strategic thinking, and woefully ignorant of the art of bidding. It's a recipe for failure of epic proportions.

To believe that winning tenders requires no proficiency in bidding is akin to believing that writing a book guarantees instant millionaire status. While anyone can attempt to write, only a select few achieve extraordinary success. Likewise, while

Beware of the folly of these misguided souls who believe they can conquer the world of tenders without mastering the art of bidding.

Their journey is a testament to the depths of human stupidity, a cautionary tale reminding us all that excellence is born from dedication, expertise, and an unwavering commitment to continuous improvement.

Hilarious Blunders of Irrelevance

Ah, the art of bidding, where hilarity ensues as some folks stumble upon the landmines of irrelevance. It's a comedy of errors that highlights the importance of understanding buyer needs, having the right mindset, and avoiding the pitfalls of brief and uninspired responses.

One common misstep is the lazy reliance on previous responses without customizing them to fit the specific question at hand. Oh, the missed opportunity! These businesses fail to connect the dots, leaving the buyer scratching their head in confusion. After all, procurement professionals are not mind-reading machines, and expecting them to recall every word you've uttered in previous pages is like expecting a goldfish to remember its multiplication tables. Errors happen, my friends, and you better be prepared for them!

To avoid falling into this trap, it's crucial to tailor each response to the question, crafting a bespoke masterpiece that aligns with the buyer's needs and the requirements of the contract. Picture yourself as a smooth-talking salesperson, reminding the buyer at every turn why you're the crème de la crème of

suppliers. Show them the magic behind your solution, ticking all those metaphorical boxes like a boss.

But wait, there's more! Recycling content from previous responses might seem like a clever time-saving trick, but alas, it can backfire faster than a faulty firework. Many bidders have learned this lesson the hard way, losing points faster than a clumsy juggler dropping bowling balls. Remember, my dear bidders, no matter how similar the questions may appear, each response must stand on its own, tailored to the tender's requirements.

Now, here's where the comedy takes an unexpected turn. Top bidders, the true jesters of the game, seize this golden opportunity to indirectly address their competitors' weaknesses and highlight their own strengths. Oh, the sweet dance of one-upmanship! With strategic improvisation, they turn their weaknesses into strengths, making their rivals' strengths seem as trivial as a rubber chicken and their weaknesses utterly unforgivable.

It's a comedy act that requires finesse and timing. Like a skilled performer on stage, these bidders know how to deliver the punchlines that leave the audience—ahem, the buyers—in awe.

Ignorance is Bliss – You Think?

In the wacky world of bidding and tendering processes, there's a group of extraordinary bidders who hold the secret to success. But here's the catch: they have to continuously improve their experience, knowledge, and skills (CPD). It's like bidding boot camp meets a comedy show!

Now, picture this: most businesses out there don't bother collecting feedback for their tender proposals. And even if they do, they ask once and give up if they don't get a response. Cue the laughter track! It's like they're playing a game of hide-and-seek with improvement.

But here's the punchline: without feedback, their performance and results stay stuck in a time warp, or worse, they nosedive. Whether they win or lose a tender, it's vital for these bidders to get detailed feedback every time. And I mean every single time!

You won't believe what happened to this one company we know. They failed not once, but twice to win a tender. But instead of throwing in the towel, they did the unthinkable. They asked for feedback and actually listened! Talk about a comedy of errors turned triumph.

Of course, there are some buyers who couldn't care less about providing feedback. They're like the silent jesters of the bidding world, toying with the hopes of bidders. But our heroes, the top bidders, don't back down. They persistently pursue those buyers, through phone calls, emails, LinkedIn messages, faxes, and even letters in the post. It's like a slapstick routine of relentless follow-ups!

In this absurd bidding circus, continuous improvement isn't just a suggestion—it's the golden ticket to winning and dominating the game. So, bidders, never miss an opportunity to obtain feedback. And if you need to, go ahead and sprinkle some humor into your pursuit. After all, in the comedy of bidding, persistence and laughter are the keys to success!

The Corporate Vampire: Tales of the Predatory Profiteer

In the murky underworld of the business realm, an ominous and manipulative figure lurked, unseen yet omnipresent, known only as The Devil. This was no ordinary competitor. He bore the charm of a thousand salesmen and the cunning of a fox. His intricate plots of intrigue were unparalleled, his schemes masterfully woven with threads of deception and temptation.

His methodology was simple yet lethal. He would ensnare unsuspecting competitors, lure them in with enticing promises of collaboration and shared triumph. Like a predator, he would make his move, enticing them with promises of shared glory. They would walk into his trap, allured by the sheen of mutual benefit, only to realize far too late the true cost of their agreement.

Once ensnared, he would cleverly extract their pricing strategies, feeding off their market knowledge and business acumen. Like a vampire feeding on the lifeblood of his victims, The Devil would drain their competitive vitality, leaving them as mere shells, depleted and hollowed, their former vigour vanished into the market's abyss.

With the gleaned intelligence and new market strategies in his possession, The Devil would weave a grand web. His intricate network of deception would glisten with the illusion of tantalising offers and advantageous deals. Like flies to a spider's web, unsuspecting procurers would be drawn in, captivated by the gleaming opportunities. They would fall into his trap, ensnared and powerless against the cunning tactics of their unseen captor.

The captured prey would be presented with an irresistible 'gift', an offer too enticing to refuse. Bewitched by the allure of a bargain, the procurers succumbed to the spell, signing agreements and contracts with the elusive Devil. Unbeknownst to them, they had entered into a dance with the most dangerous of partners.

From the shadowed corners of the market, The Devil began orchestrating his symphony of deception. His narrative, compelling and dramatic, subtly pushed for price increases. With each stroke of his conductor's baton, prices rose, and profits swelled. Within the first year alone, he managed an astonishing feat - a profit increase of 20%.

But The Devil was far from satisfied. His insatiable greed propelled him to continue this cycle, driving prices upward year after year, squeezing every drop

of potential from his ensnared procurers. By the end of the contractual period, he was gorging himself on profits that were 65% greater than initially anticipated.

The drained procurers were left reeling, their resources exhausted, their vitality depleted. The Devil had feasted well, his hunger for success temporarily sated. But his insatiable appetite demanded more.

Before venturing into his next conquest, he would collect a trophy, a symbol of his victorious deceit. A member of the procurement team, ensnared and manipulated, would give a glowing testimonial, their praises captured in a haunting video that The Devil would brandish as a weapon in his next devious campaign.

The cycle of manipulation, deceit, and vampiric exploitation would then repeat, a never-ending saga of twisted commerce in the underworld of business. The market was his hunting ground, his victims many, and the puppeteer, the entity known only as... The Devil, was always lurking, ready for his next unsuspecting prey.

Embracing the Art of Devilish Bidding

Welcome to the thrilling conclusion of our journey through the shadows of procurement. We've delved deep into the realm of "devilish" bidding, exposing the tactics that can send shivers down the spine of your competitors and procure the biggest contracts.

What we've learned is not for the faint of heart. Winning in this cutthroat world requires embracing an unconventional mindset, one that is not afraid to exploit the vulnerabilities of procurers and offer irresistible propositions. Yet, we also recognize the importance of maintaining professional ethics and ensuring value for all parties involved.

In the world of procurement, content is king. Crafting bids with substance, innovation, and value is a far more potent weapon than obsessing over perfect grammar or sentence structure. While this may seem chaotic, it's the chaotic bids that tend to stand out in the sea of monotony. So, unleash your inner maverick and create bids that are as unique as they are valuable.

Remember, the key to a successful bid is not deception, but understanding the needs of the procurers and tailoring your proposals to meet and exceed those expectations. Adopt the mindset of a

'devilish' bidder, offering irresistible value propositions and compelling narratives that align with the procurers' goals.

Dare to venture forth into this realm of high-stakes bidding and procurement. Imbue your proposals with a touch of devilish charm, outsmart your competitors, and win the heart of the procurers.

Join us in the exciting world of devilish bidding. If you're ready to take the plunge, we're here to guide you every step of the way. Send me an email at smile.marketingprojects@outlook.com and let's start a conversation on how you can gain a competitive advantage in your bidding process.

May your journey be one of success and prosperity, free from the clutches of deceptive competitors. So, here's to embracing the chaos and winning contracts faster, easier, and cheaper. The realm of procurement awaits you!

Are you ready to master the art of devilish bidding?